UNBELIEVABLE FACTS

*The World's most bizarre,
weird and amazing oddities,
facts and feats*

Geoff Tibballs

This is a Parragon Book
This edition published in 2002

Parragon
Queen Street House
4 Queen Street
Bath BA1 1HE, UK

Produced by Magpie Books, an imprint of
Constable & Robinson Ltd, London

ISBN 0-75257-789-1

A copy of the British Library Cataloguing-in-Publication Data
is available from the British Library

Printed in the EU

ACKNOWLEDGEMENTS
Illustrations courtesy of Slatter-Anderson, London
Cover photograph courtesy of Hulton Getty

CONTENTS

INTRODUCTION

Our hunger for knowledge has never been greater. How else can we be expected to win on *Who Wants To Be a Millionaire?* Whereas "What's everybody having?" used to be the line guaranteed to bring the pub to a standstill, these days it's just as likely to be, "Did you know that a crocodile can't stick its tongue out?" As the man says, that could be worth a lot of money to someone.

Unbelievable Facts is more than just a trivia book, however. Covering all aspects of life and death – people, sport, entertainment, nature, history, food and drink, science, geography – it contains hundreds of mind-boggling facts which seem too incredible to be true. Who would have thought that Charlie Chaplin once came third in a Charlie Chaplin lookalike contest; that a sneeze travels at over 100 mph; that there are no public toilets in Peru; that right-handed people live, on average, nine years longer than left-handers; that passing a child three times under the belly of a donkey was once believed to cure whooping cough; or that a pig's orgasm lasts half an hour?

In the words of Victor Meldrew: "I don't believe it!" Yet each fact is true, taken from reliable sources rather than the bloke in the pub who still maintains that the Earth is flat no matter what Judith Chalmers says.

So find out for yourself about the Prussian general who thought he was pregnant with an elephant, the Hollywood sex symbol who was born cross-eyed, the country where a third of funeral processions feature a stripper, the queen who executed any subject who appeared in her dreams, and the country whose main export is bird droppings. Then impress your friends with your new-found knowledge. Once you've started, you won't be able to stop . . .

WEIRD AND WONDERFUL PEOPLE

Barking Mad

Prussian Field Marshal Prince Gebhard Leberecht von Blücher, a hero at Waterloo, was convinced that he was pregnant with an elephant, fathered on him by a French soldier.

French poet Gérard de Nerval used to take a lobster for a walk on the end of a length of ribbon through the Palais Royal gardens in Paris. Not surprisingly, he ended up hanging himself from a lamp-post.

Following a series of disagreements with the Church in the 1930s, Rev. Harold "Jumbo" Davidson, rector of Stiffkey in Norfolk, found an unusual platform on which to air his grievances. He moved in to a cage at Skegness with Freddie the lion. But after a harmonious beginning, the lion suddenly turned on the rector and Davidson was so badly mauled that he died in hospital. Even his funeral was unconventional, his widow choosing to dress all in white, except for black shoes.

Terrified of meeting people, the fifth Duke of Portland built an elaborate network of tunnels beneath Welbeck Abbey in Nottinghamshire through which his carriage could pass in secret. So that he wouldn't have to talk to anybody, each door in his house was fitted with two letter-boxes — one for incoming and one for outgoing messages. Only his valet was allowed near him. In the event of illness, the Duke's physician had to wait outside while the valet took his master's pulse.

American artist James Whistler once dyed a rice pudding green so that it wouldn't clash with the walls of his dining room.

The second Baron Rothschild used to ride around the lanes of Hertfordshire in a trap, drawn by a pony and three zebras. He once took this unusual combination to London, pulling into Buckingham Palace where the lead zebra was patted cautiously by the royal family.

US Confederate General Richard S. Ewell thought he was a bird. To the alarm of his troops, he would cock his head to one side, peck at his food and emit curious chirping sounds.

In the 10th century, the Grand Vizier of Persia took his entire library with him wherever he went. The 117,000-volume library was carried by camels trained to walk in alphabetical order.

Mehmet Esirgen, a 52-year-old Turk, tried to cure his sexual impotence with a penis transplant . . . using a donkey as a donor. Three times he brought home a donkey, amputated its sexual organs and appealed in vain for a doctor to perform the operation. After the third occasion his family were so fed up with him that his son shot him in the leg.

Motor manufacturer Henry Ford was obsessed with diet. He campaigned for synthetic milk, insisting that cows were on the verge of obsolescence because they were unhygienic. He maintained that eating sugar was tantamount to committing suicide since its sharp crystals would cut a person's stomach to shreds. And he was such an advocate of soya beans that he once wore a suit and tie made from soya-based products.

Nineteenth-century naturalist Frank Buckland served up such meals as kangaroo stew, roast parrot, mice on buttered toast and stewed sea slug. He also tried to make elephant's trunk soup, but in spite of boiling the trunk for several days it was still too tough to eat.

In the later years of his life, Sir Ralph Richardson used to ride to the theatre on his motorcycle with his pet parrot, Jose, perched on his left shoulder.

Greek General Hajianestis, who led his nation in the 1921 war with Turkey, often refused to get out of bed because he thought his legs were made of sugar and were so brittle that they would collapse.

Wealthy English landowner William Beckford took a flock of sheep with him on a trip to Portugal – to improve the view from his window.

Henrietta Howland Green was the meanest woman in the world. She inherited a $6 million fortune from her father and became such a successful money-lender that she kept a balance of over $31,400,000 in one bank alone. Yet she lived in a seedy Brooklyn apartment in which the heating remained switched off even in the depths of winter. She never bothered to wash and for lunch ate nothing more than a tin of dry oatmeal which she heated on a bank's radiators. Her meanness extended to her family. Her son had to have his leg amputated because of her delay in finding a free medical clinic. When she died in 1916, she left an estate worth $95 million.

Father Denham of Warleggan in Cornwall positively hated people. He surrounded the rectory with a high, barbed-wire fence and further alienated his flock by painting the church red and blue. When parishioners stopped attending his services, he replaced them with cardboard cut-outs and continued to preach to those each week. He led a spartan life. There was no furniture in the rectory and, right up until his death in 1953, his diet consisted of just nettles and porridge.

The constant companion of legendary French actress Sarah Bernhardt was a silk-lined coffin. She not only learned her lines while lying in the coffin, she also entertained a string of lovers there.

Eighteenth-century Shropshire squire Jack Mytton was the Oliver Reed of his day. A heavy drinker, he once startled guests by riding a bear into his dining-room. When he suffered a bad dose of hiccups, his solution was to set fire to his night-shirt . . . while still wearing it. He suffered serious burns but it cured his hiccups.

Roman Emperor Caligula made his horse Incitatus a consul.

Eminent scientist Henry Cavendish was painfully shy. He built a private entrance to his London house so that he could come and go without meeting anyone, and used to communicate with his servants by notes only. On one occasion, he was so disturbed after bumping into a maid on the staircase that he immediately ordered the building of another staircase.

Frenchman Michel Lotito, known as Monsieur Mangetout, specialises in eating glass and metal. His diet has included supermarket trolleys, TV sets, aluminium skis, bicycles, beds, plates, razor blades, a coffin, and even a Cessna 150 light aircraft.

After losing a leg in a battle with the French in 1838, Mexican General Antonio Lopez de Santa Anna arranged for it to be given a state funeral. To the accompaniment of bands, the leg was solemnly paraded through the streets of Mexico City and laid to rest in a national shrine.

Howard Hughes: A Few Scenes Short of a Movie

Billionaire Hollywood film producer Howard Hughes had once dated the world's most famous movie stars, including Ava Gardner, Elizabeth Taylor, Lana Turner and Ginger Rogers. But he spent the last 15 years of his life as a recluse, during which time his behaviour become increasingly unbelievable . . .

He insisted that he and his second wife, Jean Peters, had separate bedrooms, even separate refrigerators.

As he became more and more obsessed with health and hygiene, he wouldn't allow anybody else, not even his wife, to touch his food.

His own doctor was only allowed to examine him from the other side of the room. ☞

☞ When the marriage ended in divorce, Hughes retreated to a bungalow in the desert near Las Vegas where Mormon body-guards protected him from contamination. So terrified was he of germs that the few visitors he received were forced to stand for inspection in a chalk square drawn outside the house before being allowed near the front door.

He would touch nothing without first wrapping his hand in a paper tissue.

Hughes took to storing his urine indefinitely in metal containers, dating and labelling each one.

When even the desert became too public, he began living in a succession of anonymous hotels. Each move was made in total secrecy, his entire entourage departing via kitchen exits and fire escapes in the dead of night with Hughes strapped to a stretcher.

The windows of the hotels were always darkened and taped. The only furniture was a bed, a chair and movie equipment, including a screen. He watched *Ice Station Zebra*, starring Rock Hudson, 150 times.

For days on end, he would eat nothing but ice cream, staying with one flavour until every parlour in the district had run out.

Only twice in ten years did he allow a barber to trim his hair or a manicurist to attend to his nails. The result was that his beard hung down to his waist.

Between 1961 and his death in 1976, he met just three people from the outside world.

That's Life

Catherine the Great relaxed by being tickled, preferably by young courtiers. For she was an infamous nymphomaniac, particularly as she got older.

It is estimated that you'll spend a year of your life looking for lost objects.

Austrian Adam Rainer is unique in having been classed as both a dwarf and a giant. In 1920, at the age of 21, Rainer was just 3 ft 10 in tall. But he then suddenly shot up to a height of 7 ft 1 in. The growth spurt took its toll and left him weak and bedridden. He died at the age of 51, by which time he stood 7 ft 8in tall.

The Marquis de Sade's mother was a nun.

He may have been a fearless soldier, but Napoleon was terrified of cats.

Hitler was fascinated by hands. In his library was a well-thumbed book containing drawings and paintings of the hands of famous people. He liked to show guests how closely his hands resembled those of Frederick the Great, one of his heroes. Hitler's square moustache was also believed to be a tribute — to his favourite comedian, Charlie Chaplin.

If you're right-handed, you tend to chew food on the right side of your mouth; if you're left-handed, you tend to chew on the left.

In school, Monica Lewinsky was voted by her classmates as The Girl Most Likely To Get Her Name in Lights.

Former North Vietnamese President Ho Chi Minh once worked as pastry assistant in the kitchens of London's Carlton Hotel.

Al Capone's business card said he was a used furniture dealer.

Unbelievable Facts

Queen Victoria's first act after her coronation was to move her bed from her mother's room.

Queen Elizabeth I owned the first wristwatch.

Eleanor Roosevelt, wife of US President Franklin D. Roosevelt, carried a revolver.

On average you spend two weeks of your entire life waiting for traffic lights to change.

Itimad, wife of King Almotamid of Seville, was desperate to know what snow looked like. So the king arranged for an entire hillside near Cordoba to be planted with almond trees. In spring, the falling petals turned the slopes white – the closest thing to snow that Itimad would ever see in southern Spain.

Alexander the Great ordered his entire army to shave their faces and heads. He believed that beards and long hair made it easy for the enemy to grab and cut off his soldiers' heads.

Around 1.2 billion letters worldwide are sent through the post every day. Joined together, they would make a bridge that would span the Atlantic Ocean.

Her first language being German, Queen Victoria never spoke particularly good English.

William Hague is colour-blind.

Peter the Great of Russia was obsessed with dwarfs. When two of his favourite dwarfs got married, he invited 72 more to come from the farthest provinces of his empire. The wedding feast was held at the royal palace, at which Peter provided small tables for the dwarfs and large tables for the other guests. When one of the same dwarfs died, Peter staged a lavish funeral ceremony. The tiny coffin was placed on a tiny hearse, drawn by small horses. At the head of the procession walked a priest, selected for his unusually short stature. Peter was also attracted to giants. He returned from a trip to France with a 7 ft 6 in colossus called Nicolas Bourgeois and married him to a Finnish woman of similar proportions in the hope that they would produce huge children. The plan failed but Peter continued to pay the couple an annual salary of 600 roubles and to include Bourgeois in his weird ceremonies, often dressed as a baby and paraded on strings by a team of dwarfs.

A person uses more household energy (in the form of water pumps) having a wet shave at the washbasin than he does using an electric razor.

In Roman times, firemen were entitled to punish anyone whose carelessness caused a fire, usually with a public beating on the spot.

The average person spends two years of his or her life on the phone.

Napoleon drew up his battle plans in a sandpit.

William the Conqueror was so strong that he could jump on to his horse wearing a full suit of armour.

St. Patrick wasn't Irish at all. He is believed to have been born in South Wales and never set foot in Ireland until he was kidnapped and taken there by Irish raiders.

Unbelievable Facts

The mighty Attila the Hun was only 4ft 6in tall.

Hitler was voted *Time* magazine's "Man of the Year" for 1938.

Edward VII recorded the height and weight of every caller to his home at Sandringham.

The average housewife walks four miles a year making beds.

Pope John Paul II used to be a promising footballer. He played in goal for the Polish amateur team Wotsyla.

Berengaria, wife of Richard I, never set foot in England. She was crowned in Cyprus and spent most of her eight-year reign in Italy and France.

Florence Nightingale kept a small owl in her pocket, even while serving in the Crimean War.

St. Simeon the Younger, better known as Stylites, spent the last 45 years of his life sitting on top of a stone pillar in Syria.

George I could neither speak nor write English.

The average worker in Japan only takes half his annual holiday entitlement.

The first Duchess of Marlborough saved money on ink by never dotting her i's or using punctuation.

The brutal Robespierre, who sent thousands to the guillotine during the French Revolution, was squeamish and couldn't stand the sight of blood.

When asked to name a colour, three out of five people will say red.

Edward V was king for such a short time that nobody had a chance to paint his portrait.

A woman from Worcestershire sneezed every day for 977 consecutive days.

Aztec emperor Montezuma had a nephew, Cuitlahac, whose name meant "plenty of excrement".

George VI came bottom of the class at Naval College.

About 17 per cent of humans are left-handed, roughly the same figure as for gorillas and chimpanzees.

Mongol emperor Kublai Khan had 5000 resident court astrologers.

Einstein couldn't speak fluently when he was nine, leading his parents to think that he might be retarded.

John F. Kennedy could read four newspapers from first to last page in 20 minutes.

The Duke of Windsor was so besotted with Wallis Simpson that he wouldn't let her touch used money in case it soiled her precious hands. So every day he issued her with a wad of freshly-printed bank notes.

In December 1975, a Californian man sent off 62,824 Christmas cards.

Karl Marx, the founder of Russian Communism, never set foot in Russia in his life. Born in Germany, he moved to France and then on to England where he wrote *Das Kapital* and other works.

Child care expert Dr. Benjamin Spock won a rowing gold medal at the 1924 Olympics.

When Lady Jane Grey was declared Queen of England and Ireland in 1553, only two towns accepted her. For nine days until she was deposed by Mary I, Jane was Queen of Berwick-upon-Tweed and King's Lynn.

Mao Tse-tung never brushed his teeth — on the grounds that tigers never brush their teeth either.

Queen Victoria insisted that husband Albert's clothes be laid out every day — even when he had been dead for 40 years.

Shih Huang Ti ruled China in the third century BC. He built a network of 270 palaces, linked by tunnels, and was so afraid of assassination that he slept in a different palace each night.

Dr. Billy Graham used to sell brushes door-to-door during the Depression.

Throughout his life, Abraham Lincoln was convinced that he was illegitimate and publicly defended those born out of wedlock. It was only after his death that he was discovered to be legitimate after all.

President Lyndon Johnson ran away from home at the age of 15. He didn't go back for two years.

Weird and Wonderful People

On average, we spend 12 years of our life watching TV.

George V used to have a pet parrot which he would encourage to walk across the breakfast table, much to the disgust of the queen.

During the First World War, the wife of US President Woodrow Wilson used to graze sheep on the front lawn of the White House.

The woman who has appeared most often on the cover of *Time* magazine is the Virgin Mary.

Catherine de Medici issued instructions that no woman at the French court should have a waist measuring more than 13 inches.

Walt Disney used to wash his hands every two minutes.

Before hot-water bottles became fashionable, parlour maids would be despatched to bed to warm the sheets before the master and mistress retired for the night.

At the age of 23, Aristotle Onassis, who went on to become the richest man in the world, was working as a humble dish-washer in a Buenos Aires restaurant.

Casanova spent the last 13 years of his life working as a librarian.

The youngest Pope was Benedict IX who was elected in 1032 at the age of 11.

Philippe, Duke of Orléans (son of Louis XIII of France), was forced to wear pretty dresses and play with dolls because his mother had always wanted a daughter.

Csar Nicholas II thought about building an electric fence around Russia.

Doctor, Doctor
Queen Christina of Sweden had a phobia about fleas. She ordered the construction of a tiny four-inch long cannon so that she could spend hours firing miniature cannonballs at the fleas which infested the royal bedchamber.

Queen Elizabeth I had a phobia about roses.

Stalin had webbed toes on his left foot.

The ultimate hypochondriac was William McIlroy. He suffered from Munchausen's syndrome – a continual desire for medical treatment. Over a 50-year period, he underwent 400 operations, and stayed at 100 different hospitals, using 22 aliases. In 1979, he announced that he was sick of hospitals and retired to a Birmingham old people's home. He died there four years later.

When he was 11, Boris Yeltsin blew off the thumb and forefinger of his left hand while taking apart a grenade.

Towards the end of his reign, Louis XIV's toes started to rot. One of them dropped off and was found by his valet in one of the royal bedsocks.

Nelson suffered terribly from seasickness.

Weird and Wonderful People

Nurse Florence Nightingale was a hypochondriac. She spent most of the last 56 years of her life in bed, convinced that she was suffering from terminal heart disease.

Anne Boleyn had six fingers on one hand and wore special gloves to hide the deformity. She also had three nipples.

Prince Christian of Schleswig-Holstein was blinded in one eye after being accidentally shot by Queen Victoria's son, Prince Arthur, while out hunting. So the remorseful Victoria bought him several glass eyes in different colours.

Danish astronomer Tyco Brahe wore a metal nose after he had lost the original to syphilis.

The stomach of Louis IV of France was twice the size of a normal human stomach.

In 1609, a doctor named Wecker found a corpse in Bologna with two penises. Since then, there have been 80 similar cases.

The Black Death wiped out three-quarters of the population of Europe in the 14th century.

Sigmund Freud, the father of psychoanalysis, had a morbid fear of rail travel.

When George VI was young, his legs were strapped into wooden splints every night because the royal doctors were worried that his legs weren't growing straight.

Napoleon and Hitler each only had one testicle.

German physicist Professor Philipp Lenard suffered from onomatophobia, the fear of certain names. He couldn't bear to speak, see or hear the name of Sir Isaac Newton. At the universities where he lectured, Professor Lenard would turn his back on the students whenever Newton's name had to be mentioned. A member of the class would then write the offending name on the blackboard, but it had to be rubbed out again before Lenard would continue with the lecture.

Charles Osborne of Iowa started hiccuping in 1922 while trying to weigh a pig for slaughter. He carried on hiccuping for the next 68 years, during which time he married twice and fathered eight children. Then one morning in 1990, his hiccups suddenly went. The following year he died.

Josef Goebbels, champion of the Nazi creed of selective breeding, himself had a club foot. His left leg was over three inches longer than the right.

From Here to Maternity
Hitler's mother was seriously considering an abortion, but was talked out of it by her doctor.

Mrs Feodor Vassilyev who lived in Shuya, Russia, in the 18th century, gave birth to a record 69 children.

Queen Anne had 17 children, none of whom survived her.

In 1994, an Italian woman gave birth to a boy at the age of 61.

Winston Churchill was born in a ladies' cloakroom during a dance.

A woman in Ohio gave birth to a boy weighing 23 lb 12 oz in 1879.

The world's youngest parents were aged eight and nine. They lived in China and became parents in 1910.

A Frenchwoman was born in 1869 with two pelvises and four legs. Yet she got married and had two healthy children.

A woman in Italy gave birth to twins 36 days apart.

Until the 1920s, babies in Finland were often delivered in saunas because the heat was thought to be beneficial in warding off infection.

The Chinese population has been growing at such an alarming rate that, in some areas of the country, the government now restricts couples from having more than one child.

Near the end of her reign, Queen Victoria was very weak, making family photographs an ordeal. So scared was she of dropping babies that a royal maid was secretly placed beneath her vast skirt to hold the baby firmly in place for the benefit of the camera.

Eric Idle and John Major were both born on the same day – 29 March 1943.

Prince Andrew and Leslie Ash were both born on 19 February 1960.

Manfred Mann and Geoffrey Boycott were both born on 21 October 1940.

Yoko Ono and Bobby Robson were both born on 18 February 1933.

Peter Gabriel and Stevie Wonder were both born on 13 May 1950.

John Motson and Virginia Wade were both born on 10 July 1945.

Lenny Henry and Michael Jackson were both born on 29 August 1958.

Charles Dance and Chris Tarrant were both born on 10 October 1946.

Stanley Kubrick and Danny La Rue were both born on 26 July 1928.

Marie Stopes, the famous birth-control campaigner, knew nothing about sex until she was 29.

In medieval China, it was not unusual for a mother to breast-feed her child until he or she was seven years old.

What a Coincidence

Of the eight US Presidents who have died in office, seven were elected at exactly 20-year intervals — William Harrison (elected 1840), Abraham Lincoln (1860), James Garfield (1880), William McKinley (second term 1900), Warren Harding (1920), Franklin Roosevelt (third term 1940) and John F. Kennedy (1960). The odd one out was Zachary Taylor who was elected in 1848 and died in office two years later.

A remarkable series of coincidences link the assassinations of Abraham Lincoln and John F. Kennedy. Lincoln was elected in 1860, Kennedy in 1960; both were assassinated on Fridays in front of their wives; their successors as President were both named Johnson; Andrew Johnson was born in 1808 and Lyndon Johnson in 1908; both assassins, John Wilkes Booth (born 1839) and Lee Harvey Oswald (born 1939), were killed before standing trial; Lincoln's secretary, whose name was Kennedy, had advised him against going to the theatre, and Kennedy's secretary, whose name was Lincoln, had warned him not to go to Dallas; Booth shot Lincoln in a theatre and ran to a warehouse, Oswald shot Kennedy from a warehouse and ran to a theatre; the surnames of both Presidents have seven letters; and the names of both assassins have 15 letters. ☞

☞ A few months before Lincoln's assassination, a student, on his way home to visit his parents, fell into the path of an oncoming train at a Jersey City railway station. He was rescued by an actor on his way to visit a sister in Philadelphia. The student was Robert Lincoln; the actor was Edwin Booth. It was Booth's elder brother who would shortly murder Lincoln's father.

Robert Lincoln was at the scene of three presidential assassinations. In 1865, he rushed to Ford's Theatre where his father lay fatally wounded. In 1881, he was at James Garfield's side seconds after the President had been shot. And 20 years later, he was on the point of joining William McKinley at Buffalo, New York, when he learned that McKinley too had been shot dead.

Writer Mark Twain was born in 1835, the year of Halley's comet. Twain remarked that as he had come into the world with the comet, so he would pass from the world with it. Halley's comet returned in 1910, and, sure enough, Twain died that year.

In 1678, the body of English politician Sir Edmund Berry Godfrey was found in a ditch on London's Greenberry Hill. Three men were tried for his murder. Their names were Green, Berry and Hill.

During the Second World War the British Museum in London was twice hit by German bombs, the second passing through the hole made by the first. Neither bomb exploded.

The Allied preparations for D-Day in 1944 were nearly wrecked by the *Daily Telegraph* crossword. The code name for D-Day was "Operation Overlord" and each stage had its individual code name. Neptune was the naval initiative, Omaha and Utah were the code names for two French beaches where landings were to take place, and Mulberry was the secret name for the artificial harbours to be used for supplies. Just over a month before the planned invasion date, these answers began to appear as answers in the *Telegraph* crossword puzzle. Finally on 2 June – just four days prior to D-Day – "Overlord" appeared as an answer. Security forces descended on the *Telegraph* office expecting to find a German spy. Instead they found bewildered schoolteacher Leonard Dawe, the man who had compiled the paper's crosswords for 20 years. The fact that the answers to five of his clues had matched the carefully-guarded code names had been pure coincidence.

In 1938, playwright A.J. Talbot penned a one-act comedy, *Chez Boguskovsky*, in which a man called Boguskovsky steals a painting from the Louvre in Paris. The following year, a painting was stolen from the Louvre. The thief turned out to be a man named Boguskovsky.

Buzz Aldrin's mother's maiden name was Moon. Aldrin was the second man on the Moon.

In 1898, retired Merchant Navy officer Morgan Robertson wrote a novel, *The Wreck of the Titan*, which uncannily predicted the *Titanic* disaster 14 years later. Apart from the similarity in the names of the two ships, Robertson's *Titan* was also a huge, supposedly unsinkable British liner making its maiden voyage from Southampton to New York with 3000 passengers on board. It too struck an iceberg in the North Atlantic and sank with many people losing their lives because of the shortage of lifeboats.

In April 1935, a ship named the *Titanian*, carrying coal from Newcastle to Canada, almost suffered the same fate as the *Titanic* when encountering an iceberg in the same area of the North Atlantic. Luckily, crewman William Reeves had a premonition of impending disaster and yelled "Danger ahead!" to the navigator shortly before the iceberg became visible in the darkness. Reeves was born on 15 April 1912 – the day the *Titanic* sank.

In 1812, the wife of French Marshal Oudinot was awaiting delivery of a bust of her husband, modelled by a German artist. But when it arrived, one of the plaster shoulders was badly damaged and about to drop off. A few days later, her husband had his shoulder smashed in battle.

Duane Allman of The Allman Brothers rock band was killed in a motorbike accident in Macon, Georgia, in 1971. A year later, fellow Allman Brothers' member Berry Oakley was killed in another motorbike crash just three blocks away.

When King Umberto I of Italy and his aide visited a Monza restaurant in the summer of 1900, the king couldn't help noticing that the restaurant owner was a dead ringer for him. They got into conversation and it emerged that both men were called Umberto and both had been born in the same town on 14 March 1844. Furthermore, both had been married on 22 April 1868, to a woman called Margherita, and each had named his son Vittorio. On the day of Umberto's coronation, the other Umberto had opened his restaurant. The day after their encounter, the king was saddened to learn that his double had been killed in a shooting accident. As he asked his aide to find out about the funeral, three shots rang out from an assassin's gun. King Umberto was shot dead.

In 1872, a French assassin named Claude Volbonne murdered Baron Rodemire de Tarazone. The baron's father had also been murdered 21 years previously – by a Claude Volbonne. The two killers were not related.

In 1799 an American privateer, the *Nancy*, was seized by a British warship in the Caribbean. Prior to capture, the *Nancy's* skipper, Thomas Briggs, managed to throw the ship's American papers overboard and replace them with Dutch forgeries. Charged in Jamaica with running a British blockade during wartime, Briggs looked set to go free for lack of evidence. But in the course of the trial another British warship, HMS *Ferret*, arrived in port and produced the incriminating papers. The *Ferret* had caught a large shark off Haiti and inside the shark's stomach were the papers.

The French playwright Molière died on stage while playing a hypochondriac in his own play *Le Malade Imaginaire* (*The Hypochondriac*).

For three successive seasons between 1956 and 1958, Leeds United were drawn at home to Cardiff City in the third round of the FA Cup. Each time, Cardiff won 2-1.

Three American Presidents have died on Independence Day, 4 July. John Adams and Thomas Jefferson both died on 4 July 1826, and James Monroe died on 4 July 1831.

When a boat sank while crossing the Menai Strait in 1664, the only one of the 81 passengers to survive was a Hugh Williams. In 1785, another boat sank in the same spot. The sole survivor was named Hugh Williams. And in 1820, 24 passengers drowned in a third disaster. There was just one survivor. His name? Hugh Williams.

Four of the first six US Presidents — George Washington, Thomas Jefferson, James Madison and John Quincy Adams — were 57 when they were inaugurated.

In 1975 a Bedfordshire family were stunned when a huge chunk of ice dropped out of the sky and crashed through the roof of their house. At the time they were watching a film on TV about the *Titanic*.

On 23 May 1939, the recently built American submarine *Squalus* sank off the eastern seaboard. A sister ship, the *Sculpin*, succeeded in rescuing half of the 56-man crew. The *Squalus* was subsequently salvaged and renamed the *Sailfish*. In 1943, the *Sculpin* was sunk by the Japanese who took 42 men prisoner, placing half of them on board the aircraft carrier *Cuyo*. Approaching Japan, the *Cuyo* was torpedoed by the *Sailfish* and everyone on board was killed. So the crew of the *Sailfish* had killed half of the survivors of the submarine that had come to their rescue four years previously!

Just One of Those Days

Robert Heinbaugh of Plainsville, Ohio, has the distinction of being the first person in the world to be shot by a lawn-mower . . . As he cut the grass one evening, he ran over a live bullet which went off and shot him in the foot. His wife saw the funny side and mowed the rest of the lawn herself.

Colorado police arrested a man for robbing the same store twice in one day. After the second hold-up, he told the assistant that he'd be back in a few hours to rob the place for a third time. True to his word, Steven Peterson returned . . . and was arrested by police who were still in the store investigating the second robbery.

Weird and Wonderful People

Paramedics in Kennett, Missouri, rescued a man who'd got his member stuck in the washbasin plug-hole. He had been trying to change the light bulb above the sink when he slipped and fell, accidentally lodging himself in the plug-hole. The blow left his penis so bruised and swollen that he was unable to extract it. Eventually a neighbour called the police who smashed down the bathroom door despite the embarrassed man's protestations that he did not want rescuing.

Darsun Yilmaz from Damali on the Black Sea was so distraught after being rejected by his neighbour's daughter that he decided to kidnap her. Climbing a ladder to her room, he threw a blanket over the head of the sleeping figure in the bed and carried her downstairs to his waiting car. After whispering lovingly in her ear, he pulled back the blanket to find instead that it contained the girl's 91-year-old grandmother.

Madame de Montespan, second wife of Louis XIV, once lost four million francs in half an hour at the gaming table.

When Isaac Mofokeng fled Johannesburg police in 1999, he ran to the local zoo and found himself in the gorilla enclosure. The regular inmate, Max, was distinctly unimpressed and ripped off Mofokeng's jeans, bit him on the buttock and pinned him against a wall. Mofokeng was only too happy to be rescued by the police.

In 1971, an object exhibited at a South Shields museum as a Roman coin was revealed to be a plastic token given away free by a soft drinks firm. The error was pointed out by a nine-year-old schoolgirl. The "R" which the museum had thought meant "Roma" in fact stood for "Robinsons".

When the United States opened the Panama Canal in 1920, the Secretary of State invited Switzerland to send its navy. It was subsequently pointed out to the Secretary that land-locked Switzerland has no navy.

Los Angeles attorney Antonio Mendoza spent over three hours having his mobile phone removed from his rectum. During the delicate operation, his phone rang three times. After recovering at a trauma centre from his ordeal, Mendoza explained: "My dog drags the phone all over the house. He must have dragged it into the shower. I slipped on a tile, tripped against the dog and sat down right on the thing."

A 30-year-old Colombian man trying to sneak through Paris airport customs in 2000 was found to have a boa constrictor in his pants.

When the French Revolutionaries stormed the Bastille in 1789, instead of finding hundreds of prisoners, they discovered just seven. Undaunted, the Revolutionaries decided to destroy the building — which they saw as a monument to royal power and oppression — at once. It took them three years to pull it down.

When two service station attendants in Ionia, Michigan, refused to hand over cash to a drunken robber, the man threatened to call the police. They still refused, so the robber went ahead and phoned the cops . . . who promptly arrested him.

Two Canadians looking to buy a quantity of cocaine in the Cayman Islands called the wrong number and ended up speaking to a police officer instead. The cops arranged a meet at which the pair were duly arrested.

I Have a Dream

The average person has 1,460 dreams a year.

You experience an average of four dreams a night, and in the course of that, your dreams become progressively longer. Your first dream of the night may only last around ten minutes, but your final dream will invariably last as long as 45 minutes.

In 1980 David Janssen, former star of the TV series *The Fugitive*, dreamed that he saw himself being carried out in a coffin after a heart attack. He consulted a psychic who advised him to go for a check-up. But it was too late. Two days later, Janssen died from a massive heart attack.

David Booth, a Cincinnati office manager, phoned American Airlines after having nightmares on ten successive nights about a DC-10 crash. Three days later, on 25 May 1979, an American DC-10 crashed at Chicago, killing 273 people.

Poet Samuel Taylor Coleridge dreamed the first 54 lines of *Kubla Khan* and started writing feverishly the moment he woke up. Unfortunately he was interrupted by a "person on business from Porlock". By the time his visitor had left, an hour later, Coleridge had forgotten the rest of the poem, and it remained unfinished.

King Wilhelm I of Württemberg completed the building of Rosenstein Castle in 1829, but didn't move in for another 35 years because a gypsy had predicted that the king would die there. He finally thought it safe to take up residence in the castle in 1864 and died five days later.

Italian composer and violinist Giuseppe Tartini dreamed the music for his finest work, "The Devil's Sonata".

Julia Grant, wife of US General Ulysses S. Grant, woke on the morning of 14 April 1865 with a strong feeling that she and her husband should get out of Washington as quickly as possible. General Grant had been due to attend the theatre with President Lincoln that night, but his wife insisted that he pull out. Leaving the city, the Grants passed John Wilkes Booth on his way to assassinate Lincoln at the theatre. General Grant was also found to be on Booth's hit list.

The design for the Taj Mahal appeared to Emperor Shah Jehan in a dream. An architect hired to draw up plans for the building was given a drug so that he too would experience a vision of the building before starting work.

Mid-way through a financial meeting, just before 5pm on 7 October 1571, Pope Pius V suddenly announced that there had been a Christian victory. Two weeks later on 21 October, a messenger from Venice rode into Rome with news that a Christian fleet had vanquished the Turks at Lepanto. The official report of the battle stated that victory had been confirmed shortly before 5pm on 7 October.

In May 1812 a Cornish innkeeper had a dream on three successive nights about the shooting of a leading politician in the House of Commons. He had no idea of the identity of the man in his dream but a friend said the description matched that of the Prime Minister, Spencer Perceval. Several days later, news reached Cornwall that Perceval had been shot dead in the lobby of the House of Commons.

Daft Deeds

Wearing protective bandages on his elbows and knees, Indian mystic Lotan Baba rolled along the streets of London for three miles in 1993 as part of his campaign for world peace.

In 1975, Rev. Geoffrey Howard, a parish priest from Manchester, pushed an ancient Chinese sailing wheelbarrow 2000 miles across the Sahara Desert. It took him 93 days.

Arvind Pandya of India ran backyards from Los Angeles to New York in 107 days in 1984. Six years later, he repeated the feat between John O'Groats and Land's End.

Peru's Felipe Carbonell told 345 jokes in an hour in 1993.

In 1990, Welshman Steve Briers recited the entire lyrics of the Queen album "A Night at the Opera" . . . backwards. It took him a fraction under 10 minutes.

Charles Creighton and James Hargis of Maplewood, Missouri, drove their Model A Ford roadster in reverse from New York to Los Angeles in 1930 without once stopping the engine.

Canadian Pat Donahue ate 91 pickled onions in just over a minute in 1978.

Back in 1900, Austrian Johann Hurlinger walked the 870 miles from Vienna to Paris on his hands.

Scotsman Dick Brown rode for 208 miles between Edinburgh and Dumfries in a suit of armour in 1989. It took him four days.

António Gomes dos Santos stood motionless for over 15 hours at a Lisbon shopping centre in 1988. It must have been one hell of a queue.

In 1989, Swede Bengt Norberg drove a Mitsubishi Colt on two side wheels non-stop for over seven hours.

For a $100,000 bet, wealthy playboy Harry Bensley set off from London in 1907 in his bid to push a pram around the world while wearing an iron mask. In August 1914, he arrived in Italy, having guided his pram through 12 of the 18 countries on his list. But with the end of his journey in sight, war broke out and the patriotic Bensley decided to do his bit for king and country. So the bet was cancelled.

For Better or Worse

Princess Maria del Pozzo della Cisterno was unlikely ever to forget the day of her wedding to Amadeo, the Duke D'Aosta, son of the King of Italy, in Turin in 1867. Her wardrobe mistress hanged herself; the palace gatekeeper cut his throat; the colonel leading the wedding procession collapsed from sunstroke; the stationmaster was crushed to death under the wheels of the honeymoon train; the king's aide was killed when falling from his horse; and the best man shot himself. After all that, even the cake was in tiers.

A French bride was arrested at her wedding reception in 1995 for stabbing her new husband with the knife they had just used to cut the wedding cake.

Actress Jean Acker left Hollywood heart-throb Rudolph Valentino on their wedding night.

The term "best man" dates back to the times when Scotsmen kidnapped their future brides. The friend of the groom who had excelled at the abduction was acclaimed to be the best man.

Harry Stevens, aged 103, married his cousin, 84-year-old Thelma Lucas, at a Wisconsin retirement home in 1984.

All of Henry VIII's wives were related to each other.

Between 1949 and 1981, one man notched up 104 bigamous marriages in 15 countries. The bigamist – who used so many aliases that nobody knew what to charge him as – was finally brought to justice in 1983 and sentenced to 34 years in jail. He died in 1991.

Victorian Prime Minister Viscount Palmerston was cited as co-respondent in a divorce case at the ripe old age of 79.

Louis XVI and Marie Antoinette did not consummate their marriage until seven years after their wedding.

Every day, 26,000 couples get married in China.

A Mexico City couple got married in 1969 after an engagement lasting 67 years. Both were 82 when they finally took the plunge.

Leopold II, King of the Belgians, was too ill to attend his own wedding. So for the 1853 ceremony to Marie Henrietta, the Austrian Emperor's brother, the Archduke Charles, stood in for him.

Casanova found it hard to keep track of his many lovers. He asked for the hand of a pretty girl named Leonilda, but her mother screamed and fainted when introduced to her future son-in-law. For she was one of Casanova's conquests, who had borne his child 17 years earlier. Casanova had been about to marry his own daughter.

Philip II Augustus, King of France, decided half-way through his wedding ceremony that he didn't really like his Danish bride Ingeborg after all. So immediately afterwards he had her locked away in a nunnery where she languished for years.

Unbelievable Facts

A man in Malaysia has been best man at around 1000 weddings.

Prior to the 20th century, Egyptian men preferred not to deflower their brides personally. Instead they hired a servant to undertake the chore.

6ft 2in tall Fabien Pretou towered over his 3 ft 1 in bride Natalie Lucius at their wedding in France in 1990.

George I had his wife Dorothea imprisoned for over 30 years. When he learned that she had finally died, he celebrated by going out to the theatre.

In 1976 Los Angeles secretary Jannene Swift officially married a 50lb rock. The ceremony was witnessed by more than 20 people.

Whenever movie star Joan Crawford changed husbands, she changed all the toilet seats in the house.

Saudi Arabian women literally have grounds for divorce. They can obtain a separation if their husband doesn't give them coffee.

In Anglo Saxon times, a man could divorce his wife on the grounds that she was too passionate.

In 1984, 97-year-old Simon Stern was divorced from his 91-year-old wife Ida in Wisconsin.

Harry Bidwell of Brighton was 101 when he was divorced from his 65-year-old wife in 1980.

The average US marriage lasts 9.4 years.

A bride-to-be in Crete suffered a nervous breakdown on the night before her wedding after discovering the groom, wearing her wedding dress, locked in a passionate embrace with the best man. Not surprisingly, the wedding was cancelled.

Elvis Presley proposed to Ginger Alden while he was sitting on the toilet. He died in the same bathroom before they could marry.

Impotence is grounds for divorce in 24 states in the US.

George IV got himself so drunk on the day of his wedding to Caroline of Brunswick that he had to be carried to the altar. That night, he fell asleep in the fireplace.

Movie star Eva Bartok said that none of her first three marriages was consummated. At 15 she was briefly married to an SS officer in Hungary. Then she entered into a marriage of convenience with film producer Alexander Paal so that she could get out of Hungary. And the third was to film publicist William Wordsworth, a descendant of the poet. They split up at the wedding ceremony.

The people of the Czech Republic throw peas at weddings instead of rice. And Italians throw sugared almonds.

The wedding tradition in Greece is to write the names of all the bride's unmarried female friends and relatives on the sole of her shoe. After the wedding, the shoe is examined and those whose names have been worn off are said to be next in line for a journey up the aisle.

In Uganda in 1995, 100-year-old Samuel Bukoro took the plunge and married 12-year-old Nyamihanda.

When his fiancee broke off their engagement, Abel Ruiz decided to take his own life. First, he threw himself in front of the Gerona to Madrid express train, but the train passed over him and he was treated at Gerona Hospital for nothing more than minor injuries. Undeterred, he resolved to try again later that day, this time throwing himself in front of a passing lorry. Again he was treated at the hospital for minor bruises. By now, staff there were so concerned about Senor Ruiz's mental state that they called in a priest who made him see the error of his ways. Determined to forget about his broken heart, Ruiz was discharged from the ward to start his new life and was promptly knocked down by a runaway horse. He was re-admitted to the hospital with serious injuries.

When American silent film actress Barbara La Marr died from heroin addiction at the age of 29, she had already been married six times.

Victorian critic John Ruskin was so repulsed by the sight of his wife's pubic hair on their wedding night that he swore that he would never sleep with her again.

Best man Albert Muldoon found himself married to the bride following a mix-up at a church in Ireland in the 1920s. Muldoon walked up to the altar with the groom but, instead of standing to the right of the groom, he stood on his left. Seeing Muldoon in that position, the priest addressed all of the questions to him, and Muldoon duly replied. The slip-up was only discovered when the real groom demanded to sign the register too. A second ceremony was swiftly arranged.

Great Escapes

Park ranger Roy C. Sullivan of Virginia was struck by lightning no fewer than seven times between 1942 and 1977. He lost nothing more than a toe-nail and his eyebrows. Having survived all that nature could throw at him, Sullivan committed suicide in 1983 after being spurned by a woman.

When Mount Pelée on the island of Martinique erupted in 1902, the only survivor in St. Pierre was a prisoner in the town jail.

American parachutist Eddie Turner saved his unconscious fellow skydiver in 1988 by pulling the ripcord of his parachute just ten seconds before he hit the ground.

In 1972 Yugoslav air hostess Vesna Vulovic somehow survived a fall of over six miles without a parachute after the DC-9 in which she was travelling blew up over Czechoslovakia.

Poon Lim of the British Merchant Navy survived 133 days on a raft after his ship, the *Ben Lomond*, was torpedoed in the Atlantic during the Second World War.

John Lee of Babbacombe, Devon, cheated the hangman's noose three times in 1885. Sentenced to death for the murder of his employer, Lee survived because on each occasion the trap-door on the gallows failed to open, even though the mechanism was tested before and after and found to be in perfect working order. The authorities knew when they were beaten and Lee's sentence was commuted to life imprisonment.

When a ship was wrecked off the coast of South Africa in 1865, all 29 people on board drowned. The only survivor was a pig which was washed ashore alive.

In 1996 a pair of Taiwanese lovers made a suicide pact when their parents refused to allow them to get married. But after surviving four suicide attempts – including hanging, driving their car off a cliff and jumping from a 12-storey building – the couple decided to give up.

In 1969, a Cuban stowaway, hiding in the wing cavity of an aeroplane, survived a 6000 mile flight at an altitude of over 35,000 ft in temperatures of −22°C.

A sheep was found alive after being buried in a snowdrift for 50 days in the Scottish Highlands in 1978.

On being found guilty of the murder of a Mississippi farmer in 1893, 20-year-old Will Purvis shouted at the 12 jurors: "I'll live to see the last one of you die!" The following February he was taken to the gallows but survived when the noose knot became loose and slipped over his head. Purvis earned a temporary reprieve and was sprung from jail before a second execution attempt could take place. In 1898 Purvis was pardoned, and nearly twenty years later another man confessed to the farmer's murder. Purvis eventually died on 13 October 1938 . . . three days after the death of the last juror at his trial.

Manic Monarchs

Charles VI of France was convinced that he was made of glass. So he refused to travel by coach in case the vibration made him shatter into a thousand pieces. He also fitted iron rods into his clothes in case he ever fell over and shattered.

Catherine the Great of Russia took such a liking to a primrose in the palace garden that she ordered a sentry to guard the plant day and night.

During one of his many bouts of insanity, George III insisted on ending every sentence with the word "peacock". He tried to open parliament with a speech which began "My lords and peacocks . . ." He also started wearing a pillowcase on his head and once, believing himself to be dead, wore black and announced that he was in mourning for "that good man, King George".

Henry III of France frequently appeared with a basket of small dogs hanging from his neck.

George III's finest moment was when driving through Windsor Great Park one day. After ordering his carriage driver to stop, the king walked over to an oak tree, shook hands with one of its branches and talked to it for several minutes. He thought he was talking to the King of Prussia.

Throughout her life, Princess Alexandra of Bavaria was convinced that she had swallowed a full-size grand piano as a child.

After staying at London's Ritz Hotel, King Amanullah of Afghanistan became so fascinated by English traditions that he tried to make the wearing of bowler hats compulsory amongst men in his native country.

Ludwig II of Bavaria decided to reverse night and day. He had a moon painted on his bedroom ceiling and started going on long coach drives in the middle of the night. Another of his moonlight escapades involved riding on horseback round and round the courtyard for up to seven hours at a time, pausing only to change horses. The object of the exercise was to simulate the distance of heroic journeys — like the one from Munich to Innsbruck — and the riding time was calculated accordingly.

Brother of Ludwig, King Otto of Bavaria concluded that the only way to preserve his own sanity was to shoot a peasant a day. So he began taking pot-shots at workers in the royal garden. When his aim started to improve, it was deemed prudent to load the king's pistol with blanks and for peasants to play dead.

Whenever Emperor Menelik II of Abyssinia felt unwell, he got his teeth into a good book . . . literally. For the Emperor's favourite cure-all was to eat a few pages of the Bible. He needed more than heavenly guidance in 1890 when, impressed by stories he had heard from America about the new electric chair, he ordered three . . . even though Abyssinia didn't have electricity. He ended up throwing two out and keeping the third as his throne.

Queen Juana of Spain was devastated by the death of her husband Philip in 1506. Unable to be parted from him, she refused to allow him to be buried and had his coffin accompany her wherever she went.

Military Mayhem

At the Battle of Karansebes in 1788, Austrian soldiers succeeded in wiping out nearly 10,000 of their own men. As darkness descended, a few drunken Austrians began shouting that the enemy Turks were upon them. The cry created such panic that the Austrians started firing indiscriminately at each other.

In 1757, Prussian soldiers failed to press home their advantage against the French when they mistook young fir trees for French infantrymen.

The entire Mexican army was routed in just 18 minutes by Texan troops in 1836 when the Mexican general ordered his men to take a siesta.

At the American Civil War Battle of Antietam in 1862, Unionist Major General Ambrose Burnside surrendered his overwhelming numerical advantage by ordering his men to march in single file across an exposed bridge. This strategy enabled Confederate marksmen to pick them off one by one. Only later did Burnside discover that the river beneath the bridge was so shallow it could easily have been crossed on foot.

The only instance of a navy being captured by a cavalry took place in January 1795. The month was part of the coldest winter for a century in Holland, enabling a French cavalry troop to cross the thick ice on the salt waters of the Zuider Zee and surround the Dutch fleet which was helplessly frozen in. Shocked at seeing French cavalrymen riding around their ships, the Dutch commanders had no choice but to surrender.

During the First World War, the strategic Fort Douaumont at Verdun was captured by a single German soldier after French General Chrétien (pronounced "cretin") forgot to pass on a message. His orders were to defend the fortress to the last man, but when he went on leave he forgot to tell his successor. As a result the mighty fortress was manned by just a handful of gunners who were taken completely be surprise. In fact, 20 were captured while attending a lecture!

At the Battle of Lepanto in 1571, the Turks ran out of ammunition and pelted Austrian soldiers with oranges and lemons.

The vast Inca empire which dominated South America 500 years ago was finally toppled by fewer than 200 men. Boasting an army of thousands, the Inca ruler Atahualpa lined up against Francisco Pizarro's tiny Spanish army of 180 men and 37 horses. But the Inca warriors were exhausted by years of civil war and when Atahualpa was captured, they fled in terror, unnerved by their first encounter with firearms and cavalry.

When relations with Bolivia soured in 1865, Queen Victoria ordered the Royal Navy to send six gunboats to Bolivia and sink its fleet. Her admirals pointed out that Bolivia had no coastline and therefore no fleet, so the queen sent for a map and a pair of scissors and cut Bolivia from the world.

The shortest war in history was that between Britain and Zanzibar in 1896. It was all over in just 38 minutes when Zanzibar's only warship, the ageing *Glasgow*, was sunk by two shells.

The Battle of Tanga in East Africa in 1914 was decided by a swarm of bees. Supported by untrained Indian troops, the British took on the might of the German army. All went well until, angered by the noise and bullets, the aggressive African bees emerged from their hives and chased the Indians back to the coast. The British were forced to evacuate and ended up losing over 1000 men.

The Russians invented the "dog mine" in the Second World War. The plan was to train dogs to associate food with the under-sides of tanks and so, with bombs strapped to their backs, to wreak havoc on the German Panzer divisions. Sadly, the dogs associated food solely with *Russian* tanks and forced an entire Soviet division to retreat. The master-plan was quickly scrapped.

Rotten Rulers

Catherine the Great of Russia was so outraged to discover the presence of dandruff on her collar that she imprisoned her hairdresser in an iron cage for three years to stop the news spreading.

Queen Ranavalona of Madagascar executed any of her subjects who appeared in her dreams.

Ferdinand II of Sicily was so vain that he would only permit the country to have its own postage stamps on condition that his portrait was not tarnished by an ugly franking mark.

Augustus II, who became King of Poland in 1607, fathered over 300 children, of which only one was legitimate.

Russian Csar Paul I banished soldiers to Siberia for marching out of step.

To deter unwanted flies, King Pepi II of Egypt always kept a supply of naked slaves handy, their bodies smeared with honey.

Prince Antoine I of Morocco took exception to his wife Marie's string of lovers. So he constructed straw effigies of them which he proceeded to hang in the palace courtyard. Whenever Marie went out, she was forced to pass beneath the effigies and was thus reminded of her infidelity.

Louis XIV of France hated washing and took only three baths in his entire adult life. But he loved beds and owned 413 of them.

Henry Christophe, King of northern Haiti in the late 18th century, instructed his guards to prove their loyalty to him by marching over a 200 ft-high cliff. Those who obeyed plunged to their deaths; those who refused were executed.

Henry VIII went off for a game of tennis while his wife, Anne Boleyn, was being beheaded.

When Russian ruler Peter the Great discovered that his wife Catherine had been unfaithful, he had the head of her lover, William Mons, chopped off and placed in a large jar of alcohol. Peter insisted that the jar remain on Catherine's bedside table to remind her of her adultery.

Murad IV, who ruled Turkey in the 17th century, found a highly effective way of demonstrating that smoking can seriously damage your health. He ordered that anyone caught smoking be executed on the spot, and that their bodies be left where they were slain as a deterrent to others. Murad was intolerant of many things. He once had a party of female picnickers drowned because they were making too much noise.

Louis XV's excuse for sleeping with teenage girls was that it reduced his chances of catching syphilis.

Victorious in battle, Egyptian King Menephta took home as a souvenir the penis of every dead Libyan soldier — some 1300 in all.

Gustav I of Sweden hacked the royal goldsmith to death because he had the nerve to take a day off without asking.

Henry VIII employed a groom whose job it was to wipe the royal bottom.

Chinese Emperor Shih Hu often selected dinner from his own harem. He would choose a girl, have her beheaded and then have the body served as the main course.

In 1924, Pope Urban VIII threatened to excommunicate snuff users.

George IV clipped off a tiny lock of hair from each woman he slept with and kept them in individual envelopes, each bearing the owner's name. When he died, over 7000 such envelopes were found in his bedroom.

Sultan Mustapha III of Turkey fathered 582 children, all of them boys.

Notorious for his acts of barbarism, Genghis Khan did have a more sensitive side. Once he was about to have an enemy executed when he realized that the man was an old childhood friend. So Genghis cancelled the execution and instead had the man rolled in a carpet and kicked to death.

Genghis Khan's cavalry rode female horses so that his soldiers could drink the animals' milk.

Timur the Lame was a descendant of Genghis Khan and inherited many of his less savoury personal traits. He enjoyed playing polo with the skulls of those he had killed in battle. On another occasion he had 5000 people beheaded so that he could use their heads to build a pyramid.

At the court of Louis XIV, only the king and queen were allowed to sit in chairs with arms.

Abbad el Motaddid of Seville, King of the Moors, used the skulls of his dead enemies as flowerpots.

Vlad the Impaler was the prototype for Dracula. As well as drinking his victims' blood, he forced wives to eat the cooked flesh of their husbands, and parents to eat their own children. He took his name from his fondness for wooden stakes. Between 1456 and 1476 it is estimated that he had over 20,000 of his enemies impaled on stakes.

King John employed a Royal Head Holder to counter seasickness. Whenever the king took to sea, servant Solomon Attefeld was on hand to hold the royal head steady. Attefeld's devotion was rewarded with the gift of large areas of land.

To eliminate competition for the throne, Turkish sultan Mahomet III had every one of his 19 brothers murdered.

Alfonso XIII of Spain was so tone deaf that he had to employ a servant to tell him when the Spanish national anthem was playing. That way, the king knew when he had to stand.

Queen Henrietta, wife of Leopold II of the Belgians, kept a pet llama which she taught to spit in the face of anyone who stroked it.

When Mahomet IV became Turkish ruler in 1648, he employed a scribe named Abdi to keep a diary of his reign. At the end of one particularly uneventful day, Mahomet learned that Abdi's entry was blank. So the king picked up a spear and impaled Abdi with it, telling him: "Now you have something to write about."

King Edward VI was an unruly child at school but, being royal, it was not permissible to cane him. So whenever Edward was to be punished, another boy, Barnaby Fitzpatrick, stepped forward to provide a substitute bottom. So the unfortunate Fitzpatrick took the beating while the king looked on.

Henry IV had his hair closely cropped because it was infested with head lice.

Ivan the Terrible of Russia was so pleased with the newly built Moscow church of St Basil that he blinded the two architects so that they would never be able to come up with anything better.

Having fallen out with the Archbishop of Novgorod, Ivan the Terrible arranged for the cleric to be sewn into a bearskin and hunted down by a pack of hounds.

Ironically for one who led such a blood-thirsty life, Ivan the Terrible died playing chess.

Pope Paul III had over 45,000 prostitutes on his payroll.

A Matter of Life and Death

Every year over 2500 left-handed people are killed from using products designed for right-handed people.

On average, 100 people choke to death every year on ball-point pens. And beware of toothpicks. They are the objects most often choked on by Americans.

You are more likely to be killed by a champagne cork than by a poisonous spider.

Each year, 13 people are killed by vending machines falling on them.

Respiratory disease is the major cause of death in China.

The ashes of the average cremated person weigh 9lb.

On his first voyage to the South Pacific in 1768, Captain Cook lost nearly half his crew to scurvy.

The odds of being killed by space debris are one in five billion.

The bubonic plague of the 17th century killed around two million people in a year. But it paled into insignificance beside the influenza pandemic of 1918 which wiped out 25 million.

You are more likely to be killed by a donkey than in a plane crash.

A third of Taiwanese funeral processions feature a stripper.

200 people a year die in avalanches.

It is possible to drown and not die. Technically, "drowning" refers to the process of taking water into the lungs, not the resultant death.

The life expectancy in Bangladesh is less than 50.

During the Crimean War, the British army lost ten times more troops to dysentery than to battle wounds.

The New York City morgue in the Bronx is sometimes so busy that relatives are given numbers and asked to wait in line to be called to identify the body.

A total of 55,700 Americans are injured each year by jewellery.

About 1000 people commit suicide on any one day.

Monday has been found to be the most favoured day for suicides, and April the most popular month.

Three times more men commit suicide than women. But three times more women *attempt* suicide than men.

In 16th-century China, people committed suicide by eating a pound of salt.

Over 50 billion aspirin tablets are taken worldwide every year.

Each day is longer than the previous one by 0.00000002 sec. This works out at 13 sec. each century.

Unhappy Endings

Pope Paul II died in 1471 while being sodomized by a page boy.

Straining to relieve constipation, George II fell off the toilet and smashed his head on a cabinet. He died from his injuries.

Ken Barger, 47, of Newton, North Carolina, accidentally shot himself dead in 1992 while answering the phone in the middle of the night. He went to pick up the phone beside his bed, but, half asleep, grabbed his .38 Smith and Wesson special instead. The gun went off when he pulled it to his ear.

King Charles VIII of France died as a result of his gallantry. On entering a tennis court in 1498, he bowed to his wife and allowed her to proceed first. As he brought his head up, it crashed against a low wooden beam, fracturing his skull and killing him.

Canadian lawyer Garry Hoy fell 24 storeys to his death while attempting to demonstrate the safety of a building's windows. Hoy was showing visiting law students around Toronto's Dominion Bank Tower. To illustrate how strong the windows were, he barged into a pane with his shoulder. The window gave way and Hoy ended up in the courtyard below. He was described by the head of his legal firm as "one of the best and brightest" members.

Isabelle, daughter of Charles VI of France, was a widow at the age of ten. She was only seven when she married England's 29-year-old King Richard II in 1396, and he died just over three years later.

Alexandros I of Greece died in 1920 from blood poisoning after being bitten by his pet monkey.

Roman Emperor Claudius choked to death on a feather put down his throat by his doctor to make him vomit.

Crown Prince Luis Filipe was King of Portugal for less than half an hour. In 1908, the prince was mortally wounded in the same attack that saw his father, King Charles, shot dead by an assassin. The prince survived his father by just 20 minutes but was technically king for that period.

Nicholas Breakspear who, as Adrian IV became the only English Pope, choked to death on a fly he'd accidentally swallowed.

King Alexander III of Scotland died when his horse jumped over a cliff while they were out riding at night.

The son of George II, Prince Frederick, should have succeeded him as king. But Frederick was hit by a cricket ball and died in 1715.

Alexander the Great dropped dead during a drinking contest. He was 32.

The first person to die of radiation poisoning was Madame Curie, discoverer of radium. She took no precautions against radioactivity and, even now, nearly 70 years on, her notebooks are still too contaminated to handle.

Escapologist Harry Houdini boasted that his stomach could withstand any blow. But one day a fan punched him without warning. Houdini collapsed in agony, having suffered an internal rupture. He died shortly afterwards.

Six people drowned in Southern Egypt in 1997 while trying to rescue a chicken that had fallen into a 60ft. well. An 18-year-old farmer was first to go in after the chicken, but drowned in the strong undercurrents. His sister and two brothers, none of whom could swim well, went in one by one to help him, but also drowned. Finally two elderly farmers went to help, but met a similar fate. After the six bodies were pulled from the well, the chicken was also brought out . . . alive.

In 1985, New Orleans lifeguards threw a party to celebrate a season without any drownings. As the party came to an end, one of the guests was found dead at the bottom of the pool.

American Jim Fixx, the man who started the trend for jogging, died of a heart attack while out jogging.

Viscount Palmerston died from a heart attack while having sex with a parlour maid on his private billiard table.

A guard in a US armoured van was killed in 1986 when $50,000 worth of quarters fell on him.

James II of Scotland was attacking Roxburgh when one of his own cannon exploded and killed him.

The Earl of Morton was beheaded by the very guillotine which he had introduced into Scotland.

Attila the Hun had a dozen wives but the last proved one too many. For he burst an artery and died while enjoying rampant sex with her on their wedding night.

In 1957, King Haakon VII of Norway slipped on the soap in his marble bath and struck his head fatally on one of the taps.

A New York husband became the first victim of 'Roid Rage in 1996. He was shot dead by his bedridden wife, who was recovering from haemorrhoid surgery, because he had gone on a six-hour fishing trip.

Napoleon's stomach finished up in a silver pepper pot. His shrivelled penis went on sale at a London auction room, but failed to reach its reserve price.

Michael Anderson Godwin spent years awaiting the electric chair in South Carolina before finally having his sentence for murder commuted to life imprisonment. Then in March 1989, while sitting on the metal toilet in his cell, he tried to fix his portable TV set. He bit into a wire and was electrocuted.

Rasputin's penis was hacked off after his assassination. No doubt if Rasputin had known about it, he would have been equally hacked off.

There was a Pope that never was. Stephen II was elected on 23 March 752, but died the following day. Since he was never consecrated, his name was omitted from Vatican records and given to his successor.

Pope Alexander VI died after consuming poison he had intended for his cardinals.

The second Marquis of Ripon killed 556,000 game birds in his life. Fittingly, he dropped dead on a grouse hunt in 1923, having already bagged 52 birds that morning.

Allan Pinkerton, founder of the famous detective agency, died of gangrene after tripping and biting his tongue.

Mithridates VI of Pontus in Asia Minor took small doses of poison throughout his life to develop a resistance in case anyone attempted to poison him. He built up such a strong immunity that when he tried to take his own life to foil the Roman invaders, the poison he took had no effect. So he ordered a slave to run him through with a sword.

A Chicago man who tried to break into a Chicago restaurant in 1991 through an air vent died after his coat caught on some pipes, twisted round his neck and strangled him. Two years earlier, the same man had tried to enter an off licence via an air vent but had merely succeeded in triggering the burglar alarm.

Pope John XIII was murdered by an irate husband who discovered His Holiness on top of his wife.

Following his unsuccessful attempt to snatch the English crown, James, Duke of Monmouth, illegitimate son of Charles II, was beheaded in 1685. But after the execution, the Keeper of the King's Pictures realized there was no official portrait of Monmouth. So the decapitated head was stitched back on and the dead Duke was placed in a chair to have his portrait painted by artist Sir Godfrey Kneller.

King John was killed by kindness. The townsfolk of Lynn in Norfolk were so delighted at being awarded a handsome contract by the king that they laid on a sumptuous feast in his honour. They rounded it off with his favourite dessert — peaches in cider. But he ate too much, suffered violent stomach pains and died a few days later.

An American poacher, Marino Malerba, shot a stag standing above him on an overhanging rock, and was killed instantly when the dead stag fell on him.

Félix Faure, President of France, died in 1899 while having sex in a Paris brothel. His sudden death sent the woman into shock and his penis had to be surgically removed from her.

Henry I died from eating too many lampreys — small eels.

In 1997, Robert Puelo was making a nuisance of himself in a St Louis store. When the clerk threatened to call the police, Puelo grabbed a hot dog, shoved it in his mouth and walked out without paying. Soon after, the police found him lying dead on the pavement outside the store. He had choked on the six-inch hot dog.

A 13th-century English nobleman, Fitzwaine Fulk, died from suffocation inside his suit of armour after his horse had got stuck in a mire.

Queen Eleanor, loyal wife of Edward I, was so upset to see her husband at death's door after infection had set into a battle wound that she personally sucked out all the poison. Her bravery saved the king's life but killed her.

In 1995 James Burns of Alamo, Michigan, was killed while trying to repair a farm truck. Burns got a friend to drive the truck along the road while he himself hung underneath in a bid to locate a troublesome rattle. But Burns' clothing caught on something and his friend found him "wrapped in the drive shaft".

Edmund Ironside, King of Southern England, was murdered in 1016 while sitting on the toilet. He sat down on the wooden lavatory box, blissfully unaware that an enemy knight, Eric Streona, was lurking in the pit below. Streona thrust his sword with such force up the royal passage that it became embedded in the king's bowels.

In 1983 a fierce gust of wind blew Vittorio Luise's car into a river near Naples. The 45-year-old managed to smash the car window, climb out and swim to the shore . . . where a tree blew over and killed him.

Margaret, "Maid of Norway", was nominally declared Queen of Scotland in 1286 but it wasn't until 1290 that the seven-year-old Margaret sailed from Norway to claim her new kingdom. Alas, on the journey across the North Sea, she suffered terrible seasickness and died in the Orkneys before ever setting foot on the Scottish mainland.

Sir Arthur Aston, a Royalist leader during the English Civil War, was beaten to death with his own wooden legs by Oliver Cromwell's troops.

On his death-bed, Bohemian General Jan Zizka gave instructions that his skin be used to cover a drum so that it could continue to beat out defiance to his enemies. The drum was sounded at the outbreak of the Thirty Years War in 1618, nearly 200 years after Zizka's death.

As doctors operated on the dying Caroline, wife of George II, she suddenly started laughing. One of the doctors had leaned too close to a candle and had set his wig on fire.

Czech housewife Vera Czermak was so distraught to learn of her husband's infidelity that she threw herself out of the window of her third-storey Prague apartment . . . just as Mr. Czermak happened to be walking along the street below. She landed on him, killing him instantly. But his body cushioned her fall, and she survived.

Dearly Departed

Keen to be buried in style, the tenth Duke of Hamilton spent £11,000 on purchasing a genuine Ancient Egyptian coffin. Alas when he died in 1852, he was found to be too long for the coffin and so his legs had to be cut off before he would fit inside.

Unbelievable Facts

Csar Peter III of Russia wasn't crowned until 34 years after his death. The coffin had to be opened so that the crown could be placed on his head.

When George V's body was carried through the streets of London, the crown fell from the top of the coffin and rolled into the gutter. Onlookers said it was a bad omen – and they were right. For although the crown was repaired, George's successor, Edward VIII, never got to wear it.

Anne Boleyn was buried in an ordinary box that had been used for storing arrows. She wasn't thought worthy of a coffin.

William the Conqueror was too big for his coffin. Two soldiers tried to force the body in by compressing it with their feet, but they jumped up and down with such vigour that they broke the king's back. This caused his stomach to explode.

The famous clown, Giuseppe Grimaldi, was so frightened of being buried alive that he insisted that his head be cut off before he was buried.

Richard I's heart was buried in a different place from the rest of his body.

After his death in 896, the body of Pope Formosus was dug up and tried for a number of crimes.

John F. Kennedy was buried without his brain. It was somehow lost during the autopsy.

Following sloppy work by the embalmers, George IV's body became badly swollen in the coffin. Amidst fears that it would explode through the lining, attendants hurriedly drilled a hole in his casket to let out some of the rotten air.

After the Battle of Trafalgar, Nelson's body was brought back to England pickled in a barrel of rum to stop it decomposing on the way home.

Nelson chose to be buried in St Paul's Cathedral rather than the national shrine of Westminster Abbey because he'd heard that Westminster was slowly sinking into the Thames.

Following his execution, Charles I's head was sewn back on to his body so that his family could pay their last respects. His neck bone was later stolen from the tomb by royal physician Sir Henry Halford who used it as a salt cellar!

Composer Joseph Haydn's head was stored in a Vienna cupboard for 60 years after his death. He was buried without it after two of his friends bribed the gravedigger to let them keep it. The missing head was eventually discovered after the world's longest game of Haydn seek.

Fashion Victims

In the 18th century, it was considered the height of fashion to wear false eyebrows made out of mouse skin.

English dandy Beau Brummel was so petrified of soiling his shoes on the pavement or of having a hair blown out of place that he used to order his sedan chair to be brought inside his house so that he could board it there. And he never used to raise his hat to a lady because he was worried that he wouldn't be able to replace it at precisely the same angle.

Boy George was sacked from his job at a shelf-stacker at Tesco for wearing the store's carrier bags. Tesco considered his appearance to be "disturbing".

Unbelievable Facts

Philip, Prince of Calabria, the eldest son of Charles XIII of Spain, adored gloves so much that he often wore 16 pairs at a time.

When Clark Gable removed his shirt on screen to reveal that he wasn't wearing a vest, sales of vests dropped by 40 per cent.

The ancient Egyptians used heated rollers to style hair more than 4000 years ago.

Before 1800, there were no separately designed shoes for right and left feet.

At the end of the 15th century, men's shoes had a square toe. The fashion was promoted by Charles VIII of France to hide the fact that one of his feet had six toes.

In 16th century Italy, it was the fashion for women to colour their teeth.

Emperor Field Marshal Jean Feeder Bokassa of the Central African Empire commissioned a pair of pearl-studded shoes costing £48,571 for his coronation in 1977.

A member of Queen Victoria's family gave her a bustle which played "God Save the Queen" when she sat down.

Most Panama hats are manufactured in Ecuador.

Only 20 per cent of diamonds are made into jewels.

In the royal courts of India, blue-blooded women used to change their clothes several times a day. They never wore the discarded garments again but gave them to slaves instead.

Weird and Wonderful People

The first pair of Doc Martens were made from old tyres.

Piercing nipples with rings was popular over 100 years ago.

It was considered elegant for aristocratic ladies of the 16th century to grow their pubic hair long and tie bows and ribbons in it.

In the 16th century an Englishman could be fined for not wearing a wool cap.

In their quest for an hour-glass figure, some Victorian women wore corsets so tight that they suffered broken ribs.

The French philosopher Voltaire owned 80 canes.

In 14th-century Europe, high-ranking noblemen were permitted to display their genitals beneath a short tunic. Those who preferred not to, could cover the area with a leather pouch.

In a recent survey, one in ten Americans admitted that they bought an outfit with the intention of wearing it just the once and then returning it to the shop.

Whenever James I wore a hole in his trousers, he didn't throw them out or even take them off. He simply slipped another pair on top.

Designer André Van Pier created a bra adorned with 3,250 diamonds. It cost £641,000.

Early bras were made from two handkerchiefs tied together by ribbon.

Unbelievable Facts

Imelda Marcos owned 500 black bras, one of which was bullet-proof, and about 3000 pairs of shoes.

85 per cent of women wear the wrong size bra.

False eyelashes were invented solely for Hollywood. Producer D.W. Griffith wanted to enhance actress Seena Owen's eyes for the 1916 film *Intolerance* and had a wigmaker weave human hair through a fine gauze.

Married men in France use more cosmetics than their wives.

When Louis XIV of France occupied the city of Strasbourg in 1681, he ordered its citizens to adopt French fashions within four months.

40 per cent of women have hurled footwear at men.

The average woman consumes 6 lb of lipstick in her lifetime.

Most lipstick contains fish scales.

Madonna's famous "Bullet Bra", worn during her Blonde Ambition tour of 1990, was based on an antique breastplate worn by Italian soldiers.

Elizabeth I made the wearing of hats compulsory for anyone over the age of seven on Sundays and holidays. Failure to do so would result in a fine of 3s 4d.

The plastic bits on the ends of shoelaces are called aglets.

Yul Brynner wore nothing but black for the last 45 years of his life.

Women across the world started wearing slacks after Marlene Dietrich looked good them in the 1930 film *Morocco*. What they didn't know was that director Josef von Sternberg had put Dietrich in trousers to emphasize the lesbian tendencies of her screen character.

Men didn't wear underwear until the 16th century.

The first hair perm in 1906 required the client to sit for six hours with a dozen brass curlers in her hair. Each curler weighed nearly 2 lb, making it the equivalent of wearing 48 large potatoes on her head.

When zips in clothing were tentatively introduced to Britain in the 1920s, people were worried about their reliability. To allay these fears, a huge zip was put on show at the Wembley Empire Exhibition of 1924. By the end of the exhibition, it had been zipped and unzipped three million times without catching.

Female pharaohs were unheard of in Egypt until Hatshepsut began her reign in 1502 BC. To lessen the shock, she had herself portrayed in male costume, wearing a beard and with no breasts.

François I of France hated beards with a vengeance. So he made the wearing of them punishable by death.

Some shoes in the 14th century had toes so long and pointed that the only way they could be walked in was to chain them to the wearer's knee.

Marie Antoinette was so modest that she always wore a gown buttoned right up to her neck — even in the bath.

Bargain Hunters

In 1988, a Gloucestershire bookseller paid £5575 for a lock of Lord Nelson's hair.

One of Sir Isaac Newton's teeth was sold for £730 in 1816. It was bought by a nobleman who had it set in a ring.

A Rudolf Hess toy soldier was bought at auction for £3375 in 1991.

The plaster cast from when Prince Charles broke his arm fetched £1800 at auction.

The red slippers worn by Judy Garland in *The Wizard of Oz* fetched £90,000 at auction in 1988.

The black bra which Madonna wore on her 1993 tour was sold for £4600 four years later.

A bottle of 50-year-old Glenfiddich whisky was sold to an Italian businessman for £45,200.

The body tag from the corpse of Lee Harvey Oswald, President Kennedy's assassin, fetched £3600 at auction.

The loin-cloth which Charlton Heston wore in the movie *Ben Hur* fetched £6250 in 1997.

In 1993, a two-tone, mint condition Dinky toy Foden tanker, purchased in the 1950s, was sold to a Californian for £4830.

A yo-yo signed by President Nixon fetched $16,029 at auction.

A 1965 letter written by John Lennon to this then wife Cynthia was sold for £17,250 in 1997.

A Steiff teddy bear was sold for £110,000 to a Japanese businessman in 1994.

A four-inch long lock of Beethoven's hair was sold for £4000 in 1994.

The marriage certificate of Marilyn Monroe and Arthur Miller was sold for £7500.

Crazy Collections

John Reznikoff of Stamford, Connecticut, collects the hair of dead celebrities. Included in his 100-strong collection are follicles from John F. Kennedy, Elvis Presley, Marilyn Monroe and Abraham Lincoln.

For the past 20 years, John McBride has been collecting piggy banks. He currently has over 3000 and they fill 27 shelves of his home in Wallington, South London.

James Bunce has no shortage of grill friends. He has a collection of 200 gas cookers, although there is only room for six at his house in Cirencester, Gloucestershire. His oldest cooker dates back to 1890.

Peter the Great established the Museum of Curiosities in St Petersburg where he assembled freaks of nature. Items on display included a man without genital organs, a child with two heads, a sheep with five feet, and a deformed human foetus. The caretaker of Peter's museum was a dwarf who had only two fingers on each hand and two toes on each foot and who knew that when he died he would be stuffed and put on display in the gallery.

Germany's Reinhard Hellwig collects mousetraps through the ages. He currently has around 2500.

The Mütter Museum in Philadelphia houses over 3000 objects which people have either swallowed or inhaled. They include a small metal battleship, ammunition and a pair of opera glasses.

Brenda Matthews from Sussex has a collection not to be sneezed at – 2000 handkerchiefs.

Anne Atkin of North Devon is the proud owner of over 2000 garden gnomes.

Weird and Wonderful People

American Hugh Hicks has amassed a total of 60,000 light bulbs.

Dutchman Nick Vermeulen is the man to know in a crisis. For he has built up a collection of over 2000 airline sickbags.

Leeds Castle museum in Kent houses a collection of dog collars spanning four centuries.

Schoolteacher Jennifer Woodward has collected over 100 miniature Homepride flour graders.

Lotta Sjölin of Sweden has over 300 parking meters.

Felix Rotter from Germany has collected some 6000 different teabag labels from around the world.

A museum in San Francisco has a collection of over 70 vibrators.

IT'S A MAD, MAD, MAD, MAD WORLD

Made in Britain

Law reformer Jeremy Bentham left his entire estate to London's University College in 1832 on condition that he be stuffed, dressed in his finest clothes and mounted in a chair from where he would continue to attend the annual meeting of the university's board of governors. His figure is still brought out to preside over an annual debate.

The British eat twice as many baked beans per head as Americans do.

William the Conqueror ordered that everyone should go to bed at eight o'clock.

Some 80,000 umbrellas are lost annually on the London Underground.

Nothing officially happened in Britain between 3 and 14 September 1752. This was because the country was switching from the old Julian calendar to the Western or Gregorian calendar, a move initially instituted by Pope Gregory XIII in 1582. Britain didn't get round to changing until 1752 when those 11 days went unobserved.

Because Britain lived by the Julian calendar, until 1752 New Year's Day fell on 25 March.

There are a dozen secret rivers flowing beneath London. One, the Effra, travels under the Oval cricket ground.

Berwick-upon-Tweed was officially at war with Russia for 110 years. As the border town frequently changed hands between England and Scotland over the centuries, it was usually referred to as a separate entity in all State documents. At the outbreak of the Crimean War, Britain declared war on Russia in the name of Britain, Ireland, Berwick-upon-Tweed and all British Dominions. But when the war ended two years later in 1856, the Paris Peace Treaty omitted Berwick. So Berwick was technically at war with Russia until 1966 when a Soviet official, made aware of the situation, visited the town to declare peace. The Mayor of Berwick said: "Please tell the Russian people that at last they can sleep peacefully in their beds!"

There are over 30,000 John Smiths in Britain.

Britain's first holiday camp was Dodd's Socialist Holiday Camp at Caister-on-Sea in Norfolk, which opened in 1906. Alcohol was strictly banned and any holidaymaker caught talking loudly after 11pm was thrown out. Accommodation was under canvas and anyone failing to keep his or her tent tidy was liable to a 6d fine for each offence.

When the 999 service was introduced to Britain in 1937, the buzzer which alerted switchboard operators to an emergency call was so loud that a number of girl operators fainted when they heard it. The noise level was eventually reduced by inserting a tennis ball in the mouth of the buzzer.

When the water level is very low at Ladybower Reservoir in Derbyshire, a church spire appears above the surface. It is the only visible remains of the villages of Ashopton and Derwent, both of which were flooded when the reservoir was filled in 1943.

Portugal is England's oldest ally. The Anglo-Portuguese Treaty signed in 1373 is still in force.

The town of Beverley, near Hull, was named after the number of beavers which once lived in the area.

In 1649, Oliver Cromwell abolished Christmas and declared that it was to be an ordinary working day. Anyone caught celebrating as usual was arrested.

In 1945, a flock of starlings landed on the minute hand of Big Ben and put the time back by five minutes.

Nowhere in Britain is more than 74$\frac{1}{2}$ miles from the sea.

Britain is the only country in the world which doesn't have the country's name on its postage stamps.

Under the laws of Alfred the Great, anyone caught fighting in the presence of a bishop had to pay 100 shillings in compensation. The fine rose to 150 shillings if an archbishop was present.

An old red telephone kiosk in Huddersfield was converted into a bar by a hotelier who promptly dubbed it the smallest public bar in Britain.

A three-seater outside lavatory at Bishop's Tawton in North Devon is a Grade II listed building.

Although illegal, gambling dens were all the rage in 19th-century Britain. Many dens hired an employee whose job it was to swallow the dice in the event of a police raid.

Female applicants for the original Directory Enquiry operators had to be single. They were expected to resign if they got married.

When it was built in 1286, Harlech Castle in West Wales was right on the coast. Now it is half a mile inland. This is because the land around the castle is slowly rising — part of northern Britain springing back into position after being weighed down during the Ice Age.

Two people in Britain died from an earthquake in 1580. A young apprentice was struck by falling masonry in London and a girl died of her injuries four days later.

When the miserable British weather threatened to dampen the ardour of the first nudists in the 1920s, their leading light suggested a compromise of wearing just a few clothes to keep out the cold.

In the 19th century anyone in Britain who tried to commit suicide and failed was hanged.

When the Gem cinema in Great Yarmouth opened in 1908, the local council decreed that men and women shouldn't sit together.

Spitting from Westminster Bridge was once a capital offence.

In 1859, Britain and the United States almost went to war over a pig. The pig, owned by an Englishman living on an island near Vancouver, was shot after straying on to an American neighbour's potato patch. Troops from both nations moved on to the island and remained on alert for the next 13 years while diplomats negotiated a peaceful outcome.

Back in the 16th century, it was legal for husbands to beat their wives – but not after 10pm.

The tax on a deck of playing cards in 16th-century England was 2s 6d – much more than a lot of people earned in a month.

There are more chickens than humans in England.

After the 1745 rebellion, led by Bonnie Prince Charlie, the government made it illegal for Scotsmen to wear kilts. The ban remained in force until 1832.

Although the Great Fire of London destroyed much of the city, only six people were killed.

Rudolf Hess was the last prisoner to be kept in the Tower of London.

America's Loony Laws

In Oklahoma, dogs must have a permit signed by the mayor in order to congregate on private property in groups of three or more.

In Minnesota, it is illegal to cross state lines with a duck on your head.

It is illegal to walk down a street in Maine with your shoelaces undone.

In Los Angeles, it is unlawful to hunt for moths under a street light.

In Pennsylvania, it is illegal for a man to purchase alcohol without written consent from his wife.

Unbelievable Facts

In Alaska, it is illegal to look at a moose from the window of an aircraft or any other flying vehicle. It is also illegal to push a live moose out of a moving aircraft.

In Nebraska, a parent can be arrested if his or her child can't hold back a burp during a church service. It is also against the law to sneeze in a Nebraska church. Meanwhile in God-fearing Alabama, it is illegal to wear a false moustache which causes laughter in church.

In Idaho, a citizen is forbidden by law to give another citizen a box of candy that weighs more than 50 lb.

When a man meets a cow in Minnesota, he is required by law to remove his hat.

In Texas, it is illegal to take more than three sips of beer at a time while standing.

In Huntington, West Virginia, it's legal to beat your wife so long as it's done in public on a Sunday – and on the courthouse steps.

In Ohio, women are prohibited from wearing patent leather shoes in public. In Cleveland, Ohio, it is illegal to catch mice without a hunting licence.

In California, it is illegal even to threaten a butterfly, let alone kill one.

In land-locked Oklahoma, it is illegal to catch whales. Meanwhile in California, it is illegal to shoot a whale from a car.

Should you wish to go barefoot in Texas, you should first obtain a special $5 permit.

In North Dakota, it is illegal to lie down and fall asleep with your shoes on.

By law, everybody in Vermont must take at least one bath a week.

No store in Providence, Rhode Island, is allowed to sell a toothbrush on a Sunday. But they can sell toothpaste and mouthwash on the Sabbath.

In Atlanta, Georgia, it is forbidden to dress a mannequin without first pulling down the window blinds. It is also illegal to tie a giraffe to a telephone pole or street lamp.

In Washington state, all lollipops are banned.

An unmarried woman may not parachute on a Sunday in Florida.

It is illegal to spit into the wind in Nebraska.

In Kansas, it's against the law to catch fish with your bare hands.

In Sarasota, Florida, it is illegal to sing in a public place in a swimsuit.

In Oklahoma, it is illegal to get a fish drunk. You also risk arrest, a fine or a jail sentence if you are caught making "ugly faces" at a dog.

In 1838, the city of Los Angeles passed an ordinance which required a man to obtain a licence before serenading a woman.

Unbelievable Facts

You may not eat cottage cheese after 6pm on a Sunday in Tampa Bay, Florida.

In California, it is illegal to peel an orange in your hotel room.

In a town in Oklahoma, it is forbidden to put a hypnotized person in a display window. And in Clinton, Oklahoma, it is illegal to "molest an automobile".

In Milwaukee, residents must keep pet elephants on a leash while walking them on public streets.

In Atwoodville, Connecticut, it is illegal to play Scrabble while waiting for a politician to speak.

In West Virginia, no children may attend school with their breath smelling of "wild onions".

In Mobile, Alabama, it is illegal to howl at ladies inside the city limits.

An optimistic law in Washington state reads: "It is mandatory for a motorist with criminal intentions to stop at the city limits and telephone the chief of police as he is entering the town."

In Muncie, Indiana, it is illegal to carry fishing tackle in a cemetery.

In Chicago, it is illegal to go fishing while wearing pyjamas.

It is strictly against the law to allow lions to run wild on the streets of Alderson, West Virginia.

In Alabama, it is illegal to be blindfolded while operating a vehicle.

In Oklahoma, a law has been passed making it illegal to take a bite out of someone else's hamburger. The state also says that it is a crime to have the hind legs of a farm animal in your boots.

In New York, a fine of $25 may still be levied for flirting. This old law prohibits men from turning around on any city street and looking "at a woman in that way". A second conviction for this crime requires the offender to wear a pair of racehorse blinkers whenever he goes out!

A law at Kirkland, Illinois, forbids bees from flying over the town.

It is illegal to start a fire under a mule in Ohio.

In California, it is illegal for anyone to try and prevent a child from playfully jumping over a puddle of water.

In Connecticut, it is illegal to walk across a street on your hands.

It is forbidden to whistle under water in Vermont.

In Tulsa, you may not open a soda bottle without the supervision of a licensed engineer.

In Michigan, a man legally owns his wife's hair.

An Ohio law states that pets have to carry lights on their tails at night.

In Florida, women may be fined for falling asleep under a hair dryer. And men may not be seen publicly in any kind of strapless gown.

It is illegal to gargle in public in Louisiana.

At Greene in New York State, it is against the law to walk backwards while eating peanuts during a concert.

In Vermont, it is illegal for a woman to wear false teeth without first obtaining written permission from her husband.

It is illegal to shave while driving in Massachusetts.

A law in Helena, Montana, states that a woman cannot dance on a saloon table unless her clothing weighs more than 3 lb 2 oz.

Birds have the right of way on state highways in Utah.

In Massachusetts, snoring is prohibited unless all bedroom windows are closed and securely locked. In the same state, goatee beards are banned unless you pay a special licence fee for the privilege of wearing one in public.

In Waterloo, Nebraska, barbers are prohibited from eating onions between the hours of 7am and 7pm. Similarly in Indiana, citizens are not allowed to attend a cinema or a theatre or to ride in a public streetcar within at least four hours of eating garlic.

A law in Kansas reads: "When trains meet at a crossing, both shall come to a full stop and neither shall proceed until the other has gone."

In Illinois, it is illegal to give a lighted cigar to a pet.

In Iowa, it is illegal for a kiss to last more than five minutes.

At International Falls, Minnesota, it is illegal for a dog to chase a cat up a telegraph pole. Owners are liable to be fined.

It is illegal to carry an ice-cream cone in your pocket in Kentucky.

In Louisiana, biting someone with your natural teeth is "simple assault", but biting someone with your false teeth is "aggravated assault".

In Massachusetts, mourners at a wake may not eat more than three sandwiches.

In Chico, California, anyone caught detonating a nuclear device within the city limits faced a fine of up to $500.

Indecent Exposure

In the Lebanon a man may legally have sex with an animal, provided it is female.

In Connorsville, Wisconsin, no man may fire a gun while his female partner is having an orgasm.

In Tremonton, Utah, it is illegal for a woman to have sex with a man while riding in an ambulance.

In Oblong, Illinois, it is illegal to make love while fishing or hunting on your wedding day.

A male doctor in Bahrain may examine a woman's genitals but must not look at them directly. He is only permitted to see their reflection in a mirror.

In Ames, Iowa, a husband may not take more than three gulps of beer while lying in bed with his wife.

Hotel owners in Hastings, Nebraska, are required by law to provide a clean white cotton nightshirt for each guest. No couple may have sex in the hotel unless they are wearing these nightshirts.

In Willowdale, Oregon, no man may curse while having sex with his wife.

The penalty for masturbation in Indonesia is decapitation.

In Kingsville, Texas, there is a law against two pigs having sex on city airport property.

In Florida, it is illegal to have sexual relations with a porcupine . . . just in case anyone was tempted.

All Our Yesterdays
At the height of its power in 400 BC, the Greek city of Sparta had 25,000 citizens and 500,000 slaves.

The steroids of ancient Rome were dried boar's dung. Chariot-racers often took a drink made from the dung before major events.

During the First World War, the punishment for homosexuality in the French army was execution.

In days of old, any Japanese person who tried to leave the country was summarily executed. As a further barrier to defection, a decree issued in Japan in the 1630s banned the building of any large sea-worthy ships.

Members of the SS had their blood type tattooed on their armpits.

The tiny Pyrenean state of Andorra found itself fighting two world wars at the same time. Due to an oversight at the end of the First World War, Andorra's name was omitted from the Treaty of Versailles, meaning that the 11-man national army was still technically at war with Germany. When the Second World War broke out in 1939, it was all too much of a strain on the Andorran resources. So the country hastily signed a private treaty with Germany, finally concluding the First World War.

The Hundred Years War lasted 116 years.

February 1865 is the only month in recorded history not to have had a full moon.

Gamblers in ancient Greece made dice from ankle bones and the shoulder blades of sheep.

To strengthen a sword in Damascus, the blade was plunged into a slave.

A golden razor removed from Tutankhamen's tomb over 3000 years after his death was still sharp enough for use.

In ancient Greece an "idiot" was a private citizen or layman.

Leather money was used in Russia until the 17th century.

Louis XIX was King of France from breakfast until tea-time on 2 August 1830, at which point he abdicated.

The punishment for men who committed adultery in ancient Greece was to have a root vegetable inserted where the sun doesn't shine.

Roman Emperor Caligula was so upset by the death of his sister Drusila that he imposed a year of mourning. During this time, everyone in the empire was forbidden to dine with his family, laugh or take a bath. The penalty for transgression was death.

The armistice which ended the First World War was typed back to front. The French clerk who was taking the dictation accidentally put some of the carbon papers in the wrong way round.

The capital of Portugal was moved from Lisbon to Rio de Janeiro in Brazil between 1807 and 1821 while Portugal was at war with France.

The Chinese were using aluminium to make things as early as AD 300. Western civilization didn't rediscover the metal until 1827.

Many of the men who acted as guards along the Great Wall of China in the Middle Ages spent their whole life there. They were born there, raised there, they married there, died there, and were even buried within the wall.

Under an old Chinese law, anyone who revealed how to make silk was liable to death by torture.

The first country to abolish capital punishment was Austria, in 1787.

Barbers used to combine shaving and haircutting with blood-letting and pulling teeth. The white stripes on the red background of a barber's pole represent the bandages used in bloodletting.

In feudal Japan, the Imperial Army had special soldiers whose sole duty was to count the number of severed enemy heads after a battle.

In 1917, it was illegal to tie a male horse next to a female horse on Main Street, Wetaskiwin, Alberta.

Americana

The New York phone book had 22 Hitlers listed before the Second World War, but none after.

Every year 11,000 Americans injure themselves while trying out unusual sexual positions.

7 per cent of Americans think Elvis is still alive.

Mount Wai-'ale-'ale on the island of Kauai, Hawaii, often has 350 days of rain a year. Yet a few miles away at sea level, there is as little as 20 in of rain annually.

Measured from its base, the tallest mountain in the world isn't Everest but Hawaii's Mauna Kea, which rises to a height of 30,800 ft from the sea bed.

There is a lawsuit every 30 seconds in the US.

Between 1701 and 1708, the Governor of New York was a transvestite. Lord Cornbury, the third Earl of Clarendon and a cousin of Queen Anne, made his entrance at the New York Assembly wearing a blue silk gown, a head-dress studded with diamonds, and satin shoes. He carried a ladies' fan. A heavily built man, he made a curious sight on the streets of New York at night, dressed in a hooped skirt and powdered wig. Although married, he spent a fortune on women's clothes for himself. However Queen Anne did send him some of her cast-offs. He once left a reception given in his honour so that he could change his dress.

America's smartest man is nightclub bouncer Chris Langan. His IQ of 195 beats Bill Gates.

In 1980, a Las Vegas hospital suspended workers for betting on when patients would die.

According to a recent study, 90 per cent of Americans would describe themselves as shy . . .

In 1861, the city of Chicago was left without any police officers for 12 hours after outgoing mayor John Wentworth fired the entire police department.

Christmas didn't become a national holiday in the US until 1890.

Four out of five Americans have suffered from piles.

Hypnotism is banned by public schools in San Diego.

President Theodore Roosevelt once shook hands with 8513 people in a single day. The occasion was a New Year's Day gathering at the White House.

Although Ohio is listed as the 17th state in the US, it is technically number 47. Until 7 August 1953, Congress forgot to vote on a formal resolution to admit Ohio to the Union.

Personal letters make up only 4.5 per cent of the mail delivered by the US Postal Service.

You could drive around the US at 100mph non-stop for four years and still not cover every stretch of road. But you'd probably be arrested for speeding . . .

Every day more money is printed for Monopoly than for the US Treasury.

Jacquelyn Morrow Lewis finished second in a recent election for the Democratic nomination for the US Senate even though she was dead. She died from a heart attack a few days before the election, by which time it was too late for her name to be removed from the ballot paper. She went on to poll 21 per cent of the vote.

Nearly half of all American bank robberies take place on a Friday.

The United States gets through enough water in one day for every American to take 64 baths. The average water consumption for the rest of the world is only a third of that of the US.

At the outbreak of the First World War, the US Air Force consisted of just 50 men.

45 per cent of Americans admit to peeing in the shower.

Mount Whitney, the highest peak in the US outside Alaska, and Zabriskie Point in Death Valley, the lowest point in the US, are less than 80 miles apart.

The *Boston Nation*, a newspaper published in Ohio during the mid-19th century, had pages which were 7½ ft long and 5½ ft wide. It needed two people to hold it aloft for reading.

Despite the number of rat-infested slums in the city, only 311 New Yorkers are bitten by rats in an average year. However 1519 citizens are bitten annually by fellow New Yorkers!

Benjamin Franklin wanted the US national bird to be the turkey rather than the eagle. He considered the eagle to be "a bird of bad moral character".

97 per cent of all paper money in the United States contains traces of cocaine.

Contrary to popular belief, Florida is not the most southerly state in the US. Hawaii is actually further south.

In an average year, over 300 Americans undergo surgery to have their buttocks lifted.

The United States bought Alaska from Russia for just two cents an acre.

While the Hiroshima atomic bomb was being prepared in New Mexico, applicants for menial jobs at the plant didn't get the job if they could read. This was because the US authorities didn't want staff reading secret papers or discarded litter.

Around 40,000 Americans have had themselves insured against being kidnapped or eaten alive by aliens.

The state of Florida is bigger than England.

Only two people signed the Declaration of Independence on 4 July 1776 – John Hancock and Charles Thomson. The majority of the other members of Congress signed on 2 August, although the final signature wasn't added for another five years.

100,000 cubic ft of water pours over Niagara Falls every second.

William Howard Taft, US President from 1909, was so fat that he once got stuck in the White House bathtub. After his release, he ordered a new one – large enough to hold four people.

The amount of junk mail that Americans receive in a day could produce enough energy to heat a quarter of a million homes.

Around 70 million Americans go jogging every day.

Barking Sands Beach on the Hawaiian island of Kauai has sand that barks like a dog. The dry sand grains emit this strange sound when walked upon in bare feet.

If a US family had two servants or less in 1900, census takers recorded it as "lower middle-class".

There are 1,525,000,000 miles of telephone wire strung across the US. There are more phones in New York City than there are in the whole of Spain.

Every 45 seconds, a house catches fire somewhere in the United States.

The parents of Dwight D. Eisenhower, who rose to become one of the few five-star generals in American history, were both pacifists.

Over 26 billion dollars in ransom money has been paid out in the US over the past 20 years.

Although the United States has just five per cent of the world's population, it has 70 per cent of the world's lawyers.

36 per cent of Americans say God has spoken to them.

The highest point in Pennsylvania is lower than the lowest point in Colorado.

Nearly 6000 men died building the Panama Canal.

25 per cent of Americans think Sherlock Holmes is a real person.

On a clear day, you can see five states from the top of the Empire State Building in New York City – New York State, New Jersey, Connecticut, Massachusetts and Pennsylvania.

There are more analysts in the US than postmen.

John F. Kennedy's assassination wasn't treated as a federal crime. In 1963, it fell under local jurisdiction.

There are no clocks in Las Vegas casinos.

There are 17 miles of corridor in the Pentagon.

Two out of five American women dye their hair.

More than 6000 shipwrecks lie at the bottom of the Great Lakes.

There is sand in Alaska. An area along the Kobuk River in the north-west of the country is a desert with dunes over 100ft high.

Richard Nixon has received more votes than any other person in US history. His three Congressional terms, two terms as Vice-President, his narrow defeat by John F. Kennedy in 1960, his run for the Governorship of California, his first election to the Presidency in 1968 and his landslide defeat of George McGovern four years later, all make Tricky Dicky the most voted for politician in the US.

A quarter of all Americans believe in ghosts.

The Inuit of northern Canada have over 20 different words for "snow", but none for "time".

Former President Lyndon Johnson's family all had the initials LBJ – Lyndon Baines Johnson, his wife Lady Bird Johnson, and children Linda Bird Johnson and Lucy Baines Johnson. The family dog was Little Beagle Johnson.

By the end of the American Civil War, between a third and a half of all paper currency in circulation in the country was counterfeit.

The Bible is the most shop-lifted book in the US.

Twenty-three sets of brothers were among the 1,177 men killed on the USS *Arizona* at Pearl Harbour in 1941.

Since 1800, soil erosion has robbed the USA of an area of land the size of Texas and New Mexico put together.

The annual expenditure on prostitutes in the US is estimated at $20 billion.

Out of Africa

If all the bends in the River Nile were straightened out, it would flow from the Equator right up to the Scottish Highlands.

The construction of the railway bridge between Mombasa and Lake Victoria at the end of the 19th century was delayed by the fact that lions killed and ate 28 of the workers.

Some 450 million years ago, the South Pole was situated where the Sahara Desert is now.

There is more uncultivated land in North America than in Africa. Some 38 per cent of North America is wilderness, compared to just 28 per cent of Africa.

The Great Pyramid in Egypt contains enough stone to build a 10 ft high wall around France. Now there's a thought . . .

The country with the biggest percentage of female heads of household in the world is Botswana.

The Nile is the only river in the world that has its source near the equator and from there flows into a temperate zone. Other rivers flow in the opposite direction.

Prevailing easterly winds carry nearly 700,000 tons of sand and dust from the Sahara Desert into the Atlantic Ocean every day.

In 1928, Liberian president Charles King swept to victory by 600,000 votes in a general election – a remarkable result considering that at the time Liberia only had 15,000 registered voters.

Over 1000 different languages are spoken in Africa. Somalia is the only African country where everyone speaks the same language – Somali.

Some sand dunes of the Sahara are higher than America's tallest skyscrapers.

As a result of the movement of the Earth's crust, the pyramids of Egypt have shifted two and a half miles to the south of where they were originally built some 5000 years ago.

Only three countries in the world are bigger than the Sahara Desert – Russia, Canada and China.

When Dutch settlers first landed in South Africa in 1632, they were so puzzled by the local dialect that they called the people around the Cape "stammerers" or Hottentots.

The Kalahari Desert in southern Africa covers an area larger than France.

It would take about 70 camels standing on each other's backs to reach the top of the Great Pyramid at Giza in Egypt.

One-time ruler of Egypt, Mohammed Ali, created two infantry regiments manned entirely by one-eyed soldiers.

Pole to Pole

The South Pole is a desert environment with roughly the same monthly rainfall as the Sahara.

In 1956, an iceberg spotted in the Antarctic was so big that it would have covered Belgium.

The windiest place on Earth is Commonwealth Bay in Antarctica. Wind speeds of 200 mph have been recorded there.

Antarctica is the only continent without reptiles.

If you sailed directly south from the Icelandic capital Reykjavik, the next land you would encounter would be Antarctica.

In some places the Antarctic icecap is almost as deep as a stack of 15 Eiffel Towers.

A census in 1920 revealed that fewer than one Eskimo in 46 had ever seen an igloo.

More people fill an American football stadium for one game than have ever been to Antarctica. Yet Antarctica is nearly twice the size of the US.

A Taste of the Orient
The Chinese were the first to use toilet paper.

Despite having a population of over a billion, China has only about 200 family names.

Singapore means "city of lions", but none have ever been seen there.

A spot in the north-west of China is 1645 miles from the nearest open sea.

Chewing gum is illegal in Singapore.

20 per cent of all publications sold in Japan are comic books.

Unbelievable Facts

A zoo in Tokyo closes for two months of the year so that the animals can have a rest from visitors.

Kettle drums were once used as currency on a remote Indonesian island.

The Great Wall of China is so large that it can be seen from space.

The Great Wall of China is 3,977 miles long – just ten miles shorter than the longest unbroken frontier in the world, that between Canada and the USA.

Venetian blinds were invented in Japan.

A school in the Philippines has 25,000 pupils.

At Tokyo's Keio Hospital, 30 per cent of outpatients diagnosed with throat polyps gave the cause as singing karaoke.

When Krakatoa erupted in 1883, the roar could be heard 2500 miles away.

The flag of the Philippines is the only national flag that is flown differently during times of peace and war. The flag is primarily blue and red halves. In peacetime, the blue half is flown on top; and during war, the red half is flown on top.

Down Mexico Way

At its peak, enough water passes along the Iguaçu River and over the Iguaçu Falls on the Brazil-Argentina border to fill six Olympic swimming pools every second. But in some years rainfall in the area is so low that the river dries up completely.

Mexico City is sinking at a rate of 18 inches per year as a result of draining the water table for human consumption.

The Panama Canal is the only place in the world where you can see the sun rise over the Pacific and set over the Atlantic.

The Amazon carries one fifth of all the fresh water that drains down the rivers of the world. It discharges enough water per minute into the Atlantic Ocean for everyone in the world to have a nice deep bath every 44 minutes.

The waters of the Amazon can be detected flowing over 100 miles out to sea.

At over 4000 miles, the Amazon is longer than the distance from New York to Berlin.

Parts of the Atacama Desert in northern Chile have had no rain for over 400 years.

Mexico once had three presidents in a single day.

The Angel Falls in Venezuela are nearly 20 times higher than the Niagara Falls.

Voters in an Ecuador village once voted a foot deodorant as mayor. As election posters sprung up around the area, the enterprising manufacturer of foot deodorant Pulvapies added one of his own: "Vote for any candidate, but if you want well-being and hygiene, vote for Pulvapies." The electors were so impressed that they duly elected Pulvapies into office.

There are 700 islands in the Bahamas, but only 30 are inhabited.

Brazil got its name from the nut, not the other way around.

The uninhabited Bouvet Island in the South Atlantic is 1050 miles from the nearest land, making it the remotest island in the world. And even the closest land — Queen Maud Land in Antarctica — is also uninhabited.

The Bolivian capital, La Paz, is virtually fireproof. Situated at 12,000 ft above sea level, there is barely enough oxygen to support combustion.

The Amazon has 1100 tributaries.

Duelling in Paraguay is legal as long as both parties are registered blood donors.

There are no public toilets in Peru.

Quirky Customs

The women of one South Pacific tribe are obliged to marry at birth.

The Masai warriors of Kenya consider it the height of good manners to spit at each other. They also leave their dead relatives out in the bush for hyenas to eat.

The Xhosa women of Africa are allowed to smoke pipes when they come of age.

Every July, Alaska stages a moose-dropping festival, dedicated to all things that come from a moose's bottom. You can buy jewellery and fancy goods — all made from moose droppings of course — and there is a contest where competitors toss gold-painted moose droppings at a target.

The men of the Walibri tribe of Australia greet each other by shaking penises rather than hands.

The Caramoja tribe of Northern Uganda tie a weight on the end of their penises in an attempt to make them longer.

In Fiji and New Guinea, it used to be the custom for widows to be strangled or buried alive with their recently-deceased husbands. The idea was that they could then join their spouses in the next life.

The most predictable race in the world is the statue race which takes place during the Festival of Candles at Gubbio in northern Italy. Every May, statues of St Ubaldo (who once saved the town from invasion), St George and St Anthony are paraded through Gubbio on top of 30ft poles before being raced up the nearby 2690ft high Monte Ingino. Since the track up the mountain is too narrow for overtaking, the result hasn't varied since the event's inception. St Ubaldo always wins, followed by St George and finally St Anthony.

Nepalese women demonstrate their love for their husbands by washing the feet of their menfolk and then drinking the dirty water.

The women of ancient Greece used to count their ages from the day they were married rather than the day they were born. It was thought that life only began for women once they were married.

The people of the Andaman Islands in the Pacific do not use fire.

The Running of the Sheep Festival at Reedpoint, Montana, is a gentle alternative to Spain's Running of the Bulls. Each September hundreds of sheep charge down Main Street for six blocks. Contests are held for the ugliest sheep and prettiest ewe.

To make guests feel comfortable, Eskimo men used to lend them their wives.

The Mazateco Indians of Mexico can conduct an entire conversation simply by whistling.

The Mambas of the New Hebrides wrap their penises in yards of cloth to make them look a foot and a half long.

Victorian ladies were told never to place books by male and female authors next to each other on their library shelves unless the authors were married.

The men of the Mandam tribe of North American Indians had to go through the most painful initiation ceremonies before they could count themselves as real men. First they had to fast for four days — they weren't even allowed to drink. Then, using a selection of serrated knives, the chief medicine man carved slices of flesh from their chests before thrusting wooden skewers into the gaping wounds. Leather thongs were attached to the skewers and the men were hoisted from the floor by the thongs. Heavy weights were attached to the legs and the men were spun round and round in circles. If they survived all this, they were given a hatchet with which they had to hack off the little finger of their left hand. The tribe was wiped out by illness in the 1840s!

A tribe from Borneo keep their dead in huge earthenware jars. As the corpse rots, the bodily fluid is drained away and the dried remains are put in a smaller container. The original jars are then re-used for cooking.

The Spanish town of Buñol hosts La Tomatina, a 90-minute mass brawl involving some 200,000 lb of ripe tomatoes. The festival dates back to 1944 when the town fair was ruined by hooligans throwing tomatoes at the procession.

In ancient Egypt, priests plucked every hair from their bodies, including eyebrows and eyelashes.

Unbelievable Facts

Animals are taken to church services on St Anthony's Day in Mexico. The saint is asked to protect the pets who are decorated with ribbons for the occasion. In rural regions, peasants take bags of insects and worms to be blessed in church, in the hope that this will prevent them from damaging drops.

Eskimos never gamble.

Amongst the ancient Egyptians and Chinese, widows used to have their tongues tattooed as a way of demonstrating their grief to others.

Every church in Malta has two clocks showing different times. This is to confuse the Devil about the time of the next service.

Norway stages an annual grandmothers' festival where grannies ride motorbikes and racehorses and go skydiving and scuba-diving. The star of the inaugural event in 1992 was 79-year-old Elida Anderson who became the world's oldest bungee-jumper.

According to Indian folklore, The Day of the Dead is when the deceased return to life. Every 2 November, Mexicans mark the occasion with macabre graveside picnics. The ghoulish gourmets sit in cemeteries and tuck into such delights as chocolate coffins, sugar wreaths, and fancy breads decorated with skull and crossbones.

In northern Siberia, women demonstrate their love for a man by showering him with slugs and lice.

The World About Us

If the history of the Earth were to be measured in proportion to one year, man did not appear until 8.30pm on 31 December.

Only 29 per cent of the Earth's surface is dry land.

About one-tenth of the Earth's surface is permanently covered with ice.

If the ice caps melted completely, the sea level across the world would rise by around 250 ft – enough to put Big Ben under water.

The average iceberg weighs 20 million tons.

If all of the people in the world today stood shoulder to shoulder, they would fit on the small Indonesian island of Bali. The island measures 2,240 square miles.

Every ten minutes, another plant or animal life form becomes extinct.

There are over 500,000 earthquakes in the world every year. Of these, 100,000 can be felt and 1000 cause damage.

In the course of history, over 75 million people are estimated to have been killed by earthquakes.

Just under a quarter of the land area of the world is desert.

The Pacific Ocean covers nearly a third of the globe. It contains more water than all the world's other oceans and seas put together.

Unbelievable Facts

Only one-ninth of an iceberg is above water.

The canopy of a rainforest is so thick that only one per cent of sunlight reaches the ground.

The longest mountain range in the world is under water. The Mid-Ocean Ridge extends about 40,000 miles from the Arctic Ocean via the Atlantic to the Pacific off the west coast of North America.

Although the Earth's crust consists of solid rock, if you were to break it down into its component elements, nearly half of it would vanish into thin air. This is because 46.6 per cent of the Earth's crust is made up of oxygen.

Over 100 tons of cosmic dust fall to earth each day.

Every 2,000 years, a lump of space debris the size of a block of flats hits Earth.

If you gave everyone in the world the same size piece of land, each person would get approximately 100 sq ft.

It is estimated that millions of trees in the world are accidentally planted by squirrels who bury nuts and then forget where they hid them.

The energy released in one day by the eruption of some volcanoes is 800,000 times as powerful as the Hiroshima atom bomb.

Ninety per cent of all volcanic activity takes place underwater.

Wish You Were Here?

When an earthquake shook Lisbon in 1755, the shock waves could be felt as far away as Loch Ness.

More than 25 per cent of the world's forests are in Siberia.

Over 800 different languages are spoken on Papua New Guinea.

Every day, 8.5 million tons of water evaporate from the Dead Sea.

The shoreline of the Dead Sea is the lowest place on Earth. If the Empire State Building were situated on the shore of the Dead Sea, only the top of its mast would actually be above sea level.

Bird droppings are the chief export of the Pacific island of Nauru.

Nauru is the only country in the world with no official capital. Its government offices are all in the Yaren District but no single place has been declared the capital.

The first municipal dump in the world was in Athens, around 500 BC.

New Zealand was the first country to give women the vote, in 1893.

The Nullarbor Plain of Australia covers 10,000 square miles without a single tree.

Unbelievable Facts

In the Falkland Islands, there are 350 sheep for every person.

The city of Istanbul straddles two continents – Europe and Asia.

Tonga once issued a postage stamp in the shape of a banana.

Roads on the Pacific island of Guam are made with coral. Guam has no sand, all the "sand" on the beaches being ground coral. So this coral sand is used for mixing concrete rather than going to the expense of importing real sand from other countries.

Only around 35 per cent of Iraqi women are literate.

The St Gotthard road tunnel under the Swiss Alps is almost twice as long as the height of Mt Everest.

There are twice as many kangaroos in Australia as people.

Bath water in Australia flows around the plug-hole in an anti-clockwise direction.

Mount Everest is 1 ft higher than it was in 1900.

There is a law still on the books in Milan which requires citizens to smile at all times in public or risk a hefty fine. Exemptions include visiting patients in hospital or attending funerals.

The glue on Israeli postage stamps is certified kosher.

Australia is the fifth largest country in the world but its population is smaller than that of Seoul, the capital of South Korea.

More capital cities begin with B than any other letter.

Every Swiss citizen is required by law to have access to a bomb shelter.

There is only one tractor in the entire country of Tuvalu in the Pacific Ocean.

As recently as 1974, more people went to East Germany for their holidays than to Greece.

The average depth of the North Sea is only 180 ft. The average depth of the Pacific is nearly 14,000 ft.

An undersea river, the Cromwell Current, flows eastward beneath the Pacific for 4000 miles along the equator. It is 190 miles wide and is 1300 ft deep in places. Its volume is 1,000 times that of the Mississippi.

The Berlin bunker where Hitler committed suicide is now a car park.

The principality of Monaco is smaller than New York City's Central Park.

India has a Bill of Rights for cows.

There are more post offices in India than anywhere else in the world.

You don't have to pay to post letters in Andorra.

There are 158 verses in the Greek national anthem.

A gold nugget found in Australia in 1869 weighed over 150 lb — as much as a grown man.

Internet access in Burma is restricted by anti-modem laws. Illegal possession of a modem can lead to a prison term.

The Canary Islands were named after dogs, not birds. In Roman times, the islands were known for the wild dogs which roamed there. The Latin word for "dog" is "canis" and so they were christened the Canary Islands. When explorers visited the islands in the 16th century, they brought home pretty little singing birds which they had found there and which they duly named "canaries".

A church in the Czech Republic houses a chandelier made of human bones.

An estimated 120 million cubic feet of snow fell in an avalanche in the Italian Alps in 1885.

In Bhutan, all citizens become a year older on New Year's Day.

Six million years ago, the Mediterranean was a desert. But then the Atlantic Ocean burst through the strip of land connecting Europe and Africa to form the new sea.

There are nearly 850 different dialects in India. Of the population of over 850 million, only around 160 million understand Hindi.

The first letter of every continent's name is the same as the last — Africa, America, Antarctica, Asia, Australasia and Europe.

The only two countries whose names start with an "A" but don't end with an "A" are Afghanistan and Azerbaijan.

There are more Maltese people in Melbourne, Australia, than there are in Malta.

In Bangladesh, pupils as young as 15 can be jailed for cheating in exams.

The smallest island in the world to have country status is Pitcairn in Polynesia. The main island measures just 1.75 sq miles.

New Zealand has more pipe bands per head than any other country in the world.

There are no turkeys in Turkey.

As a result of movement in the Continental plates, Iceland is getting bigger each year. And it's estimated that in a million years' time, the Atlantic will be 25 miles wider than it is today.

Until 1984 Belgians had to choose their children's names from an official list of 1500 drawn up in the days of Napoleon.

The Maldives has the highest marriage rate per head in the world.

In most countries, if you nod your head it means "yes". But in Bulgaria and Albania, it means "no".

Unbelievable Facts

Estonia has more accidents per head than any other country.

New Zealand is the only country which has every climate in the world.

In Turkey the colour of mourning is violet, not black.

There is a place in Norway called A . . . one in Japan called O . . . and one in France called Y.

There is also a town in Norway called Hell . . . and one in Newfoundland called Dildo.

Canada banned national beauty contests in 1992, saying they were degrading to women.

No woman or female animal is permitted to set foot on Mount Athos in Macedonian Greece.

Women in Iceland don't change their surname when they get married.

The people of Liechtenstein once held a referendum to decide where a public toilet should be situated.

Chasing a chicken through town naked used to be the punishment for a Frenchwoman who had committed adultery.

For 2000 years, the distance a cow's moo travelled was used as a unit of measurement in India.

There are no rivers in Saudi Arabia.

Barmy Beliefs

Tickling was outlawed in some ancient middle eastern countries because it was thought to be an aphrodisiac.

The ancient Egyptians thought that the world was created when it hatched from the egg of an ibis.

In 18th-century England it was widely believed that if a wealthy woman married a man with debts, the creditors would be unable to reclaim their money from her as long as she was married naked.

John Lennon believed that the number 9 affected everything in his life. He and son Sean shared a birthday of 9 October. Future manager Brian Epstein first attended a Beatles concert at the Cavern in Liverpool on 9 November 1961 and clinched a record deal with EMI on 9 May 1962. The group's first record, "Love Me Do" was on Parlophone 4949. Lennon met Yoko Ono on 9 November 1966 and thought it significant that their New York apartment was on West 72nd Street and their Dakota home was no. 72 (7+2 = 9). Similarly, he placed great store by the fact that, as a student, he had taken the no. 72 bus from his home to Liverpool Art College. This fixation sometimes manifested itself in his songs which included such titles as "Number 9 Dream", "Revolution 9" and "One After 909", written at his mother's house – 9 Newcastle Road, Wavertree. Lennon was shot dead by Mark Chapman late on the evening of 8 December 1980 in New York but the five-hour time difference meant that it was 9 December in Liverpool. His body was taken to the Roosevelt Hospital on Ninth Avenue.

Composer Arnold Schoenberg was superstitious about the number 13. He died on Friday the 13th at 13 minutes to midnight.

Italian motor racing driver Alberto Ascari was another who was fearful of the number 13. He also used to become hysterical at the sight of a black cat and would refuse to drive past one. Instead he would turn his car around and seek an alternative route. Luckily for him, he didn't come across any on Grand Prix circuits.

When Princess Margaret was born in 1930, the registration of her birth was delayed so that her number on the register would not be 13.

The Persians thought that human tears could cure a variety of ailments. So they used to bottle them for future use.

Elizabethan women used to think that drinking a puppy's urine would do wonders for their complexion.

The number 4 is reckoned to be unlucky in Japan because it's pronounced the same as "death".

The Romans thought it was bad luck to enter a house left foot first.

In Iceland it is believed that an unmarried woman who sits at the corner of a table won't marry for seven years.

It used to be considered unlucky to cut your nails on a Sunday.

When conducting, Tchaikovsky used to hold his chin with his left hand because he was afraid his head would roll off his shoulders.

Benito Mussolini used to touch his testicles in order to ward off the evil eye. At least that was his story.

The Japanese believe that picking up a comb with its teeth facing your body brings bad luck.

In parts of Romania, they used to think it was dangerous for someone to sleep with his or her mouth open. They believed that the person's soul, in the shape of a mouse, would run out of the open mouth and escape. If the mouse didn't return, the sleeper could never wake up.

In the Middle Ages, people believed that a vegetable could scream. It was thought that if a person dug up a mandrake – a poisonous relative of the potato – it would scream, and that the person responsible would die shortly afterwards.

In Indonesia, it is considered good luck if a gecko – a small lizard – barks while a child is being born.

Everyone in the Middle Ages thought that the heart – not the brain – was the seat of intelligence.

In the wake of the deaths of her husband and daughter, California rifle heiress Sarah Winchester was told by a medium that their lives had been taken by spirits and that unless she built a mansion to house the spirits, she too would die. Another stipulation was that the building work must never be completed and so for the next 38 years, right up until her death, Mrs. Winchester feverishly added rooms to her house. By the time she died in 1922, it had 160 rooms, 2000 doors, 10,000 windows, 47 fireplaces and miles of secret passages and corridors, many of which led nowhere. She was also obsessed by the number 13. So she had her house built with 13 bathrooms, there were 13 hooks in every cupboard and 13 candles in every chandelier. In the sewing-room, she insisted on there being 13 windows and 13 doors. There were even 13 parts to her will, which she signed 13 times.

You could tell the time by George II. At one minute to nine every night, he would stand outside his mistress's bedroom, fob watch in hand. At precisely nine o'clock, he would enter, pull down his breeches and have sex – often without removing his hat.

The ancient Greeks believed that the womb had two compartments – one for girls, the other for boys.

Nigerians believe that a man hit with a broom will become impotent unless he retaliates seven times with the same broom.

The Greeks believed that if a couple had sex while the wind was blowing from the north, they would have a boy. A southerly wind was supposed to produce a girl.

Edward VII had been told by a palmist that the numbers 6 and 9 would guide his life. His names – Albert and Edward – each had six letters and he had been born on the ninth day of the month. He married in 1863 (when split this makes 9+9) to a bride, Alexandra, whose name had nine letters, as did that of her father, Christian IX. Edward's coronation took place on 9 August and he reigned for nine years before dying at the age of 69.

In some regions of France the locals still believe that if a bachelor steps on a cat's tail, he won't find a wife for at least a year.

The Dutch believe that people with red hair bring bad luck.

In Ibiza it is thought to be bad luck to allow a priest on to a fishing boat.

Charles Dickens always touched things three times for luck.

Greek philosopher Aristotle thought that animals were created from a mixture of mud and rotting flesh.

George V deliberately kept the hundreds of clocks at Sandringham 30 minutes fast so that he'd never be late for an appointment.

Shelf Lives

In Australia, Scotch tape used to be known as Durex.

The world's most famous perfume was created in 1921 by Frenchman Ernest Beaux who submitted various samples to fashion queen Gabrielle "Coco" Chanel. She chose the fifth sample and so promptly named it No. 5. That had always been her lucky number anyway and, taking no chances, she launched the new perfume on the fifth day of the fifth month (May).

One of the best-selling chocolate bars in Sweden is called Plopp.

Avon cosmetics came about because the people of America rejected the Lord. Back in the 1880s, young David H. McConnell spent his school vacations selling Bibles. But he soon realized that the small samples of perfume which he gave out with the good book were received with greater enthusiasm than the Bibles themselves. So he founded the California Perfume Company, the forerunner of Avon.

There is a brand of lawn fertilizer in Japan called Green Piles.

Kleenex tissues were originally designed as make-up removers until customers pointed out that they were also ideal for nose-blowing.

Tupperware's air-tight seal nearly proved its downfall. Shop assistants were unable to prise the containers open for demonstration.

Marigold rubber gloves are made with the same technique as Durex.

For the past decade, artificial Christmas trees have outsold real ones.

Pledge, as in the furniture polish, means "piss" in the Netherlands.

TCP was originally invented as a cure for venereal disease.

When Kevin Keegan was managing Newcastle United, he advertised Sugar Puffs on TV. As a result fans of north-east rivals Sunderland refused to buy the product. Sainsbury's in Sunderland reported a 20 per cent drop in sales of Sugar Puffs.

Throughout the world, some 15 million BiC Crystal ball-point pens are sold every day. Put together, they would be capable of drawing a line half-way to the Sun.

The French have a brand of soft drink called Pshitt.

Strange Structures

The only solid walls in Philip Johnson's Glass House are in the bathroom. The rest of the house in New Canaan, Connecticut, is completely transparent, although there are sliding panels should the homeowner require privacy.

In the heart of the Australian outback near Ayers Rock is a hotel built in the shape of a crocodile.

The dome on Monticello, once the home of former US President Thomas Jefferson, conceals a billiard room. In Jefferson's day, billiards was illegal in Virginia.

Unbelievable Facts

The top part of an 18th-century lodge in Dunmore Park, Scotland, is built in the shape of a pineapple.

Since steel expands in heat, the Eiffel Tower is six inches higher in summer than in winter.

The Triangular Lodge at Rushton in Northamptonshire was built in homage to the Holy Trinity. Everything about the building relates to the number three. It has three sides, each of which measures 33 ft. There are three gables on each side, it has three storeys and triangular or hexagonal rooms decorated with trefoils or triangles in groups of three. All of the Latin inscriptions have 33 letters.

The Colosseum in Rome was built from 292,000 cartloads of stone.

The major tourist attraction at Margate, New Jersey, is a hotel in the shape of an elephant. The six-storey Elephant Hotel has its reception area in the hind legs.

The smallest house in Britain is a 19th-century fishermen's cottage at Conwy in North Wales. It consists of two tiny rooms and a staircase and measures just over 8 ft from front to back.

Each year there is one ton of cement poured for every man, woman and child in the world.

The Tokyo head office of contraceptive manufacturer Fuji Latex is built in the shape of a condom.

The Empire State Building weighs less than the earth which was excavated for its foundations.

In 1931, industrialist Robert Ilg built a half-sized replica of the Leaning Tower of Pisa outside Chicago, and lived in it for several years.

Back in the 1st century AD, the Roman emperor Augustus imposed a height limit of 80 ft on tower blocks within the city.

The ten-room Ice Hotel in Lapland offers the ultimate in cold comfort. Built entirely from snow and ice, the average room temperature is −4°C. The beds are made from packed snow. There is even a small sub-zero chapel for weddings — the perfect place to say "I d-d-d-do". Guests are advised to book early as the hotel melts every April and has to be rebuilt the following winter.

Unlike most skyscrapers, Chicago's Mercantile Exchange Building was built without an internal steel skeleton. Apparently it relies on the thickness of its walls to stay up.

Although George Washington oversaw the construction of the White House, he never actually lived there.

Most of the population of the South Australian town of Coober Pedy live underground. Some homes were converted from old opal mines but others have been dug out specifically as residences. They offer protection from the hot days and bitterly cold nights. The town also boasts The Desert Cave, Australia's first underground five-star hotel.

There are over 10 million bricks in the Empire State Building.

A team of Canadians built a 21 ft 6 in high sand castle in 1993.

A house in Rockport, Massachusetts, is made entirely from recycled newspaper. The walls have 215 reinforced layers of newsprint. Not surprisingly, smoking is prohibited inside.

Within the space of a few months in 1923, Scotsman Arthur Furguson succeeded in selling three different London landmarks to gullible American tourists. He sold Big Ben for a £1000 deposit, Buckingham Palace for £2000 and Nelson's Column for £6000.

Back in the 19th century, St Enodoc Church at Daymer Bay in Cornwall was almost completely submerged by sand blown in from the nearby dunes. The only way in was through the roof and that was how the vicar got in every Christmas to fulfil the requirement that a vicar had to enter his church at least once a year.

Ever since it was built in 1972, the 60-storey John Hancock Tower in Boston, Massachusetts, has suffered from windows suddenly popping out and shattering on to the street below. The John Hancock Mutual Life Insurance Agency tried to remedy the problem by replacing all 10,334 windows with 400 lb sections of tempered glass, but still windows continued to smash for no apparent reason. So now the company hires two permanent guards who do nothing but patrol the street and look out for cracked panes before they come crashing down on to passers-by.

Jules Undersea Lodge is an underwater hotel, five fathoms down in the Florida Keys. A converted underwater research station, it has a restaurant and two rooms, both with private baths, and can cater for six guests at a time.

In Washington, DC, it is illegal to have a building taller than the Capitol.

The Sultan of Brunei's palace has 1788 rooms and 257 toilets. The underground garage accommodates the Sultan's 150-plus cars.

The main library at Indiana University sinks over an inch every year. When it was built, engineers failed to take into account the weight of all the books that would be housed in the building.

THE NAME OF THE GAME

Fantastic Feats

American golfer Maud McInnes took 166 strokes at a par-3 hole in 1912 after her tee shot landed in a river. As the ball floated away, she climbed into a boat and tried to play out on to dry land. She eventually succeeded a mile and a half downstream.

Identical twins John and Desmond Rosser scored holes-in-one in consecutive rounds while playing at New Zealand's Auckland Golf Club in 1975.

American boxer Daniel Caruso psyched himself up before a 1992 fight by pounding his gloves into his own face before the introductions. Unfortunately he overdid it and broke his nose. The doctor ruled Caruso unfit to box.

Disorientated by the wheeling of a scrum, Brunei rugby player Dick Dover ran 75 yards to touch down unchallenged . . . beneath his own posts.

Competing in the 1979 Pan-American Games, Wallace Williams of the Virgin Islands was so slow that by the time he had reached the stadium, it was locked and everyone had gone home.

In 1914, J.N. Farrar accepted a bet that he could complete a round at Royston Golf Club in under 100 . . . while carrying full infantry equipment, including rifle, haversack, field kit and water bottle. He shot a 94.

Unbelievable Facts

Australian golfer Rufus Stewart played 18 holes in total darkness in 1931 without losing a single ball. He went round in 77.

Australian swimmer Fanny Durack once held every women's world record in the sport from 50 yards to a mile.

The 1972 Bandama Motor Rally in West Africa was so tough that nobody finished.

James Carvill completed 18 holes of the 6154-yard Warrenpoint Golf Course, County Down, in just over 27 minutes in 1987.

A Danish rugby union match in 1973 saw Comet beat Lindo 194-0.

Preparing to take on Al Couture at Lewiston, Maine, in 1946, boxer Ralph Walton was knocked out while still adjusting his gum shield in his corner. The fight officially ended after 10½ seconds – and that included the 10-second count.

At Woking Golf Club in 1972, two players finished their match all square despite not halving a single hole. The odds against that happening are 1,413,398 to 1.

Mexican skier Roberto Alvarez finished so far behind in the cross-country event at the 1988 Winter Olympics that worried officials sent out a search party to look for him.

Rick Sorensen completed 18 holes of Meadowbrook Golf Club, Minneapolis, in 86 strokes . . . even though he was blindfolded. Unfortunately it wasn't enough to prevent him losing $70 on a bet.

In 1976, Greece's Dimitrion Yordanidis finished a marathon in Athens in 7hr 33min. He was 98.

In 1971, Nicolette Milnes-Walker, a 28-year-old research psychologist at the University of Wales, sailed the Atlantic single-handed . . . and in the nude.

A golfer in Massachusetts got a hole in one after his ball stopped on the rim of the cup but was helped in by an earth tremor.

The fight between Mike Collins and Pat Brownson at Minneapolis in 1947 lasted just four seconds. Collins floored his opponent with the very first punch and the contest was stopped without a count.

In 1935, athlete Jesse Owens set six world records in 45 minutes. At 3.15pm, he shattered the world 100 yards record; ten minutes later, he set a new standard for the long jump; at 3.45 he broke the record for both the 220 yards and 200 metres; and at 4pm, he smashed the record for the 220 yard and 200 metre low hurdles.

In the men's singles final of the 1987 All-England Badminton Championships between Morten Frost of Denmark and Indonesia's Icuk Sugiarto, there were two successive rallies of over 90 strokes.

In the face of searing heat at the 1950 Tour de France, Abd-El Kader Zaag drank a bottle of wine and promptly fell off his bike. After sleeping it off by the roadside, he climbed back in the saddle and sped off – in the wrong direction.

Golfer Jack Nicklaus holed a 110 ft putt at the 1964 Tournament of Champions.

Playing at Rickmansworth Golf Club over Easter 1960, Mrs Paddy Martin achieved three holes in one – on Good Friday, Saturday, and Easter Monday. All three came at the 125-yard 3rd hole with the same club and ball.

Diana Gordon-Lennox of Canada took part in the slalom and downhill at the 1936 Winter Olympics despite having to ski with one arm in a plaster cast.

Cuban postman Felix Carvajal would have won the bronze medal in the 1904 Olympic marathon had he not stopped to pick unripe fruit from an orchard. The indigestion relegated him to fourth.

A golfer in Ontario saw his tee shot come to rest on the edge of the hole. Just as he was cursing his luck, a butterfly landed on the ball and toppled it into the cup for a hole in one.

Soccer Shorts

A Manchester City fan was banned in 1995 from bringing dead chickens into City's Maine Road ground. He used to celebrate City goals by swinging the birds around his head.

In 1957, the Salisbury and District FA of Rhodesia officially approved the payment of £10 to hire a witch doctor. Salisbury had lost every match the previous season.

Striker Elisha Banda, who played for Zimbabwe airforce team Cone Textiles, was kidnapped, drugged and tortured for eight days by team-mates angry that he'd signed for a civilian team. He was found bound and gagged on scrubland outside Harare.

The Name of the Game

There are only two football teams on the Isles of Scilly – the Gunners and the Wanderers. They play each other every week in the league, the only break being when they meet in the Cup.

In 1973, the entire Galilee team spent the night in jail for kicking their opponents during an Israeli League game.

Stopping off en route to Iceland, the Albanian national team were thrown out of England in 1990 after going on a shopping spree at Heathrow. They had thought "duty free" meant help yourself.

Italian referee Marcello Donadini was taken to hospital in 1973 after being bitten in the back by a player who didn't agree with a decision.

Barcelona's Hristo Stoichkov was banned for six months in 1990 for stamping on the referee's foot after being sent off in a Cup tie against Real Madrid.

The Liberia team escaped imprisonment by holding Gambia to a goalless draw in 1980. The Liberian Head of State, Master Sergeant Samuel Doe, had threatened to jail them if they lost.

Bolton arrived for a match at Middlesbrough in the 1940s without any shin pads. So their trainer went out and bought 22 paperback romantic novels as temporary replacements.

West Ham defender Alvin Martin scored a hat-trick against three different goalkeepers in the 8-1 win over Newcastle in 1986. The injured Martin Thomas was replaced in the Newcastle goal first by Chris Hedworth, then by Peter Beardsley.

Unbelievable Facts

A referee at a friendly match in Brazil drew a revolver and shot dead a player who disputed a penalty decision. The referee escaped on horseback.

Hollingsworth Juniors football team from Manchester fell victim to an own gull in a match with Stalybridge Celtic Colts in 1999. Colts were leading 2-1 when 13-year-old striker Danny Worthington tried a speculative shot from 25 yards. The ball was sailing way over the bar until it hit a passing seagull on the head, spun over the Hollingsworth goalkeeper and landed in the net. Despite protests, the goal was allowed to stand. Realizing they were up against 12 men, demoralized Hollingsworth went on to lose 7-1.

The Scottish Cup tie between Falkirk and Inverness Thistle in 1979 was postponed no fewer than 29 times because of bad weather.

The first Littlewoods Pools coupon attracted the interest of just 35 punters.

The Sampdoria team and 200 players walked 20 miles to a mountain sanctuary near Genoa in 1969 to thank the Madonna for helping them stave off relegation.

In 1990, the Football League banned Scarborough from wearing shirts advertising Black Death vodka on the grounds of bad taste.

Everton used to play at Anfield.

In 1998, the Macclesfield mascot was sent off for making obscene gestures during a players' brawl in the match with Lincoln City.

Cash-strapped Portsmouth cancelled their weekly order of new jockstraps in 1999, a move which would save £112. Administrator Tom Burton ordered the club to wash them instead of buying new ones.

When England entertained Malta in 1971, the match was so one-sided that the ball didn't cross the England goal-line once in the entire 90 minutes. And Gordon Banks in the England goal didn't have a shot to save.

Visitors Kilmarnock had to take the same penalty seven times during a fixture at Partick in 1945. The spot-kick was eventually saved and Partick went on to win 5-3.

Bury players refused to do any more promotional work for the club in 1997 as a protest at the lack of nappy-changing facilities at Gigg Lane for their wives.

In an attempt to boost gates, Bristol City staged a chimps' tea-party before the 1976 game with West Ham.

Plymouth Argyle striker Dwight Marshall was accidentally injured by one of his own fans after scoring at Chester in 1999.

In 1993, HFS Loans League team Congleton were forced to call off a minute's silence to mourn the death of the club's oldest fan . . . when he walked into the ground.

Referee Henning Erikstrup was about to blow for full-time with Norager leading Ebeltoft 4-3 in a Danish league match when his dentures suddenly fell out. While he scrambled around looking for them, Ebeltoft equalized. Despite vehement protests from Ebeltoft, Mr Erikstrup disallowed the goal, replaced his false teeth and promptly blew the final whistle.

A Tanzanian soccer match was postponed in 1978 after the referee was arrested on the pitch and accused of smoking marijuana just before the kick-off.

In the space of five minutes at Sunderland in November 1998, Barnsley striker Ashley Ward scored, missed a penalty and was sent off.

Leicester City went through an entire FA Cup tie with Northampton Town in 1997 without committing a single foul. Leicester won 4-0.

In 1999, a Manchester City fan threw an asthma inhaler on to the pitch during a disappointing home draw against Northampton.

Dundee United's Premier Reserve League game against Dunfermline at Arbroath in 1998 was abandoned after just 90 seconds because of high winds.

At the age of 52, Pedro Gatica cycled from his home in Argentina to Mexico for the 1986 World Cup, only to find on arrival that he couldn't afford to get in. While he was trying to haggle for a ticket, thieves stole his bike.

Giuseppe Lorenzo of Bologna was sent off after just ten seconds of the Italian League match with Parma in 1990 for striking an opponent.

Romanian midfielder Ion Radu was sold by Second Division Jiul Petrosani to Valcea in 1998 for 500 kg of pork (worth about £1750).

A 1984 match between Sheffield United and Oldham was postponed when a war-time bomb was found near Bramall Lane.

Fans at Gillingham were subjected to celery searches in 1996. A craze had started for waving sticks of celery while chanting an obscene song. So anyone caught in possession of the vegetable was threatened with a life ban.

Quick Singles

Former Prime Minister Sir Alec Douglas-Home played first-class cricket for Middlesex.

Sussex batsman H.J. Heygate was given out in a match with Somerset in 1919 because he didn't reach the crease within two minutes of the fall of the previous wicket. Poor Heygate was crippled with rheumatism.

A team of one-legged cricketers played a team of one-armed cricketers in 1863. The one-legged team prospered from their opponents' difficulties in catching the ball and won by 21 runs.

Club cricketer Lindsay Martin scored 100 off 20 deliveries for Rosewater against Warradale in 1987. He hit 13 sixes, five fours and two singles.

Surrey villagers Bookham beat the Electrical Trades Commercial Travellers Association CC in 1952 without scoring a run from the bat. The ETCTA were dismissed for 0, and then the first ball of the Bookham innings went for four byes.

The Test match between England and South Africa at Durban in 1939 was finally abandoned as a draw on the tenth day because the England players had to catch their ship home.

Players of Horsham and South Hampstead fled the pitch when a menacing-looking bull appeared on the scene, having escaped from a nearby market. The only person left out in the middle was one of the umpires who thought it was a female of the species.

The Duke of Wellington played for All Ireland against Garrison in 1792, scoring 5 and 1.

When Abdul Aziz was injured in the first innings of a match in Karachi in 1959, the scorecard read: "Abdul Aziz retired hurt . . . 0." But the injury proved to be fatal, so for the second innings the scorer wrote: "Abdul Aziz did not bat, dead . . . 0".

The First Test between Young Sri Lanka and Young England at Columbo in 1987 was held up when a large iguana crept across the wicket.

South Africa's Hugh Tayfield bowled 16 consecutive eight-ball maiden overs against England in 1957.

To liven up a dull encounter between Sussex and Leicestershire, Sussex's John Snow bowled a ball of soap at batsman Peter Marner. The scorecard recorded the resultant contact between ball and bat as: "Ball exploded."

A fielder in a match at Horncastle, Lincolnshire, was struck on the head by a hang-glider making an unscheduled landing.

Pakistan Railways beat Dera Ismail Khan by an innings and 851 runs in 1964. In reply to the railwaymen's 910 for 6 declared, Dera Ismail Khan were bowled out for 32 and 27.

Cricket in Latvia began and ended when a policeman, sent to observe the strange game from close quarters, stopped a cover drive with his head. The game was immediately banned in Latvia for being too dangerous.

Batting at Kalgoorlie, Australia, in the 1970s, Stan Dawson was struck by a ball which set light to a box of matches in his trouser pocket. He was run out as he tried to beat down the flames.

England wicket-keeper Godfrey Evans once spent 1 hr 37 min at the crease before scoring his first run. The occasion was a Test match against Australia at Adelaide in 1947. Evans went on to make 10 not out.

Despite having no left arm from the elbow down, Bob Ascough scored a century for Yorkshire club Staveley against Minskip in 1963.

Own Goals

French rugby player Gaston Vareilles missed his international debut against Scotland in 1910 . . . all because of a sandwich. When the team train stopped at Lyon, Vareilles nipped to the buffet. But the queue was so long that by the time he returned to the platform, the train was disappearing into the distance. He was never picked for his country again.

The world middleweight title fight between Jack "Nonpareil" Dempsey and Johnny Reagan on the sea front at Long Island, New York, in 1887 was abandoned after eight rounds when the tide came in and flooded the ring.

English golfer Roger Wethered missed out on winning the 1921 British Open when he incurred a penalty for accidentally treading on his ball. The additional stroke put Wethered in a play-off which he lost.

The Tunisian team competing in the 1960 Olympic modern pentathlon failed to score a single point. In the show jumping section, the entire team fell off their horses; one of their swimmers came perilously close to drowning; and they were ordered from the shooting range because of fears that they were endangering the lives of the judges. When it came to the fencing, they were severely handicapped by having only one man who could fence. Behind his mask, the Tunisians hoped that nobody would realize they were sending out the same man over and over again. But in the course of the gallant competitor's third contest, his opponent recognized him as the man he had just fought and had him disqualified.

Around $1 million is lost at US race tracks every year by punters who lose or carelessly throw away winning tickets.

The Name of the Game

In 1996, the Belgian government announced a new law banning camel and ostrich racing on the nation's public roads. A mystified spokesman for Belgium's local authorities said: "As far as we know, no one has ever tried to race camels or ostriches in Belgium."

Angry at seeing her son Tony taking a battering in the boxing ring, Mrs. Minna Wilson climbed into the ring, took off one of her high-heeled shoes and began pummelling opponent Steve McCarthy around the head with it. The referee quickly intervened, but not before Mrs Wilson had inflicted considerably more damage than her son on the unfortunate McCarthy. Bleeding from a head wound, which he claimed was the result of Mrs Wilson's soft-shoe shuffle, McCarthy refused to box on, only to be disqualified for failing to continue with the fight. To the amazement of the McCarthy camp, Wilson was declared the winner, but subsequently a re-match was ordered. And this time Mrs. Wilson was banned from attending.

Dr Sherman Thomas, a 60-year-old Maryland physician and keen golfer, was halfway through his putting backswing when he was distracted by the honking of a Canada goose. He missed the putt and sought revenge, felling the bird with a blow to the head. Up before the local beak, he was fined $500 for killing a goose out of season.

After winning a rowing gold medal at the 1956 Olympics, 18-year-old Russian Vyacheslav Ivanov managed to drop it into the lake. He dived in to try and find it, but the search proved unsuccessful.

Dozens of runners in a 13-mile half-marathon at Newton Aycliffe, County Durham, ended up doing as many as 20 miles after getting hopelessly lost in fog.

Racehorse No Bombs romped home by eight lengths in a 1979 race at Ascot, only to be disqualified for having eaten a Mars Bar beforehand. The chocolate bar contains caffeine and theobromine, two mild stimulants which are banned in the racing world.

Scottish golfer Bobby Cruickshank was so overjoyed at a slice of good luck in the 1934 Merion Open that he hurled his club into the air . . . and forgot to move out of the way when it came crashing down. Badly dazed, he carried on and finished joint third.

French rugby player Jean-Pierre Salut broke his ankle *before* the 1969 international with Scotland in Paris. About to run on to the pitch, he tripped on the steps leading up from the dressing-room.

During the 1980 Corfu International Golf Championship, Sharon Peachey saw her drive collide in mid-air with a ball from a competitor playing a different hole. Not only did Ms. Peachey lose vital yardage, but her ball ended up in a pond.

Sheikh Mohammed paid $10.2 million for racehorse Snaafi Dancer, but the horse proved so abysmal that it never even got on to a racecourse.

A rugby union match between Whitby and Corby in 1989 was abandoned because the Corby players were too drunk to continue. The referee called a halt seven minutes into the second half with Corby already losing 80-0.

Sierra Leone boxer John Coker had to drop out of the 1966 Commonwealth Games in Kingston because he couldn't find any gloves to fit him.

With both teams lined up ready for kick-off, a Welsh rugby match was abandoned in 1966 when it was realized that nobody had brought a ball.

A Canadian businessman bought a racehorse for £5000 minutes before it ran in a race in Montreal – then watched as it came in fourth and dropped dead.

With the fight ebbing away from him, a boxer in the Philippines suddenly pulled a knife from his shorts and attacked his opponent. He was then shot dead by a policeman in the crowd.

Standing on the 18th tee at a Kent golf course, club professional W.J. Robinson was confident of clearing a cow which was grazing 100 yards up the fairway. Alas, his drive clattered into the cow, killing it and leaving Robinson with what could only be described as a tricky second shot.

Italian Carlo Airoldi decided to make his way to the 1896 Athens Olympics on foot. The journey from Rome took over a month and when Airoldi eventually arrived in Greece, he was told he couldn't compete because he was a professional.

US tennis sensation Venus Williams was docked a point at the 1999 Australian Open Championships when a string of beads came undone from her dreadlocked hair and scattered all over the court.

The triumph of Luxembourg's Josef Barthel in the 1500 metres at the 1952 Helsinki Olympics was greeted with embarrassed silence. Nobody had expected a Luxembourg athlete to win a medal at the Games and so when it came to the medal ceremony, there was no sign anywhere of the score to the Luxembourg national anthem. After an awkward delay, the band struck up a hastily improvised version.

Did You Know?

The first puck used in ice hockey was a frozen piece of cow dung.

Cheetah racing was staged in London in 1937.

You took your life in your hands playing American Football in its formative years. In the 1905 season, 18 players were killed and 150 seriously injured.

The 1908 Olympics included a demonstration of bicycle polo. Ireland beat Germany 3-1.

Fidel Castro was voted Cuba's best schoolboy athlete for 1944. He had a trial for Washington Senators baseball team, but was turned down.

Olympic athlete Roger Black was not allowed to run as a schoolboy because of a heart defect.

Tennis player Lighton Ndefwayl blamed his defeat in a Zambian professional tournament on the fact that his opponent kept breaking wind.

Racehorse trainer Richard Hannon used to be drummer with the Troggs.

Before Wembley Stadium was opened, an infantry battalion and hundreds of volunteers marched up and down the terraces for 15 minutes to test their strength and safety.

Half a million rivets went into the building of Wembley Stadium.

A bowling pin need only tilt 7.5 degrees in order to fall down.

The Name of the Game

When Uganda and Kenya both took to the field in white shirts for a rugby union international at Entebbe in 1935, a lady spectator saved the day by racing on to the pitch carrying a bottle of black dye. She hastily dyed the Uganda shirts black and the game went ahead with the home team playing in wet shirts.

In 1457, King James IV of Scotland made golf illegal because his subjects were neglecting their archery practice in order to play the game.

Mary Queen of Scots was a keen golfer. She also owned one of the world's first billiard tables.

A 1956 Olympic water polo match between Hungary and the USSR was abandoned after it degenerated into an underwater brawl.

American jockey Frank Hayes was found dead in the saddle after riding Sweet Kiss to victory in a race at Belmont Park in 1925.

Johnny Herbert came fifth in the 1989 United States Grand Prix, but a local American firm refused him a hire car because he was under 25.

The stadium at Apia where the Western Samoan rugby team played home matches in 1924 had a large tree right in the middle of the pitch.

Lacrosse was first played by American Indians. Jay Silverheels, who played Tonto in the TV series *The Lone Ranger*, was a professional lacrosse player.

Over 820,000 golf balls are sold worldwide every day.

Polo was played in Persia in the 6th century BC where it was used to train cavalrymen.

Athene, dam of champion racehorse Rheingold, was so useless as a two-year-old that she was given away as first prize in a raffle.

A golf club in Arizona offers a free drop should your ball come to rest adjacent to a rattlesnake. And a club in Uganda offers a drop without penalty if the lies is lying in the immediate vicinity of a crocodile.

The Australian rugby union team's mascot on the 1908 tour of Britain was a live snake. Half-way through the tour, the snake died and the Australians immediately lost their first game, at Llanelli.

There are 336 dimples on a regulation golf ball.

Alan Stacey drove in Grands Prix for Lotus in the late 1950s despite the fact that his right leg was made of tin.

Edward VII owned a golf bag made from an elephant's penis. It was a gift from an Indian maharajah.

The United States are the reigning Olympic rugby union champions. They beat France back in 1924 – the last occasion that rugby featured in the Olympics.

Basketball was first played in 1891, but it was another two years before anyone thought of cutting a hole in the bottom of the net.

There was only one event in the first Olympic Games — a running race along the length of the stadium.

Many Japanese golfers are insured against scoring a hole-in-one. This is because, when you get an "ace", it is a Japanese tradition to share your good fortune by sending gifts to all your friends. If you're popular, this can work out pretty expensive. So the Japanese let the insurance company cough up instead.

Oddballs

Forty-eight years after winning the women's 100 metres final at the 1932 Olympics, American Stella Walsh was revealed to be a man. The secret came to light in 1980 when Walsh was shot dead during a Cleveland armed robbery.

French racing driver Jean Behra wore a plastic ear after the original had been severed in a crash in 1955. In case history repeated itself, he always kept a spare plastic ear in his pocket.

Leicestershire cricketer and lay preacher Albert Knight used to get down on his knees and pray at the crease before each innings.

When Preston beat Reading 18-0 in 1893-94, their goalkeeper Jimmy Trainor had so little to do that a wore a raincoat in the second half.

The 1912 Olympic marathon in Stockholm was run in intense heat. It all proved too much for Japanese runner Shinzo Kanaguri who dropped out after 16 miles to join a family having a picnic by the roadside.

Baseball legend Babe Ruth used to wear a cabbage leaf on his head to keep him cool. He changed it every two innings.

Canadian golfer Moe Norman once teed off in the Los Angeles Open using a Coca-Cola bottle.

An Italian racing driver of the 1920s, Giuseppe Campari, liked to sing opera during a race.

American golfer Ky Laffoon had a love-hate relationship with his putter. After one missed putt he was seen trying to strangle it and, when that failed it, he tried to drown it by holding it down under water! Finally he decided to punish it by tying it to the bumper of his car and letting it bruise itself on the tarmac on the way to the next tournament.

Desperate to boost attendances for the ailing St Louis Browns baseball team in 1951, owner Bill Veeck gave out live lobsters to fans.

After excelling in two games for a senior rugby club in New Zealand, 26-year-old stand-off Jamie Kahakura was suddenly banned when it was discovered that he was a woman.

Thomas Birch, a keeper of books at the British Museum during the reign of Queen Victoria, was a keen angler. To blend in with the surroundings and improve his chances of a catch, he used to dress in a tree costume.

Reigning Tour de France champion Pedro Delgado of Spain only finished third in the 1989 event after losing three minutes at the start signing autographs.

1930s Australian cricketer "Chuck" Fleetwood-Smith used to do bird impressions to liven up a dull game . . . often as he came in to bowl.

Wealthy racehorse owner Dorothy Paget lived life in reverse. She had dinner at seven o'clock in the morning, slept through the day (unless she was due at the races), and then got up for breakfast at 8.30pm. She then spent the night eating huge meals and telephoning her long-suffering trainers.

An Eskimo by the name of Emaku Gluco prepared for his 21-mile swim across the Catalina Strait off California by living in a fridge. He abandoned the swim half-way across, complaining that the water was too warm.

Keen to rub shoulders with Jack Nicklaus and Arnold Palmer, Barrow crane driver Maurice Flitcroft entered the 1976 British Open – even though he had never played a full 18 holes of golf. He took 121 in the qualifying round. Seven years later, he tried again, this time disguising himself as Swiss professional Gerald Hoppy. By the ninth hole of his qualifying round, he had already taken 62 strokes and was rumbled by officials who politely suggested that Herr Hoppy might care to retire.

Waving to the crowds after finishing fourth in the 1989 US Motor Cycle Grand Prix, Australia's Kevin Magee fell off his machine on the lap of honour and broke a leg.

Hearing that lunch had been put back to two o'clock, Nottinghamshire batsman George Gunn deliberately surrendered his wicket . . . just so that he could take lunch at his preferred time of 1.30.

Paulo Mata, coach with Brazilian soccer club Itaperuna, was so incensed at the award of a late goal against his team and the sending off of three players that he ran on to the pitch and dropped his trousers in front of TV cameras.

American boxer Harry Greb held the world middleweight title for three years despite being blind in one eye.

Yorkshire and England cricketer Bobby Peel was a heavy drinker. He was sacked for trying to bowl at the sightscreen (in the mistaken belief that it was an opposing batsman) and for then urinating on the wicket.

After missing two simple putts during a round in 1919, former US Open champion Chick Evans was so annoyed with himself that he holed out with the handle of his umbrella.

Playing for Sheffield United against Liverpool in 1898-99, 20-stone goalkeeper "Fatty" Foulke picked up the opposing centre-forward and stood him on his head in the penalty area mud.

Incompetent marshalling at a Belgian road race in 1988 sent the entire field of 200 cyclists speeding down a hill straight into roadworks. Over 50 riders came to grief in the pile-up.

Derbyshire batsman Harry Bagshaw was buried dressed in his umpire's coat and clutching a cricket ball.

Golfer Brian Barnes once 12-putted from just 3ft. After missing his first putt, he lost his temper and kept jabbing at the moving ball.

The legendary cricketer W.G. Grace once shocked his team-mates by suddenly declaring the innings closed with his own score on 93, just seven short of a century. He later explained that 93 was the only score between 0 and 100 that he had yet to make. On another occasion, he got a bottom edge off his bat and the ball lodged in the top of his pad. Seizing the opportunity to add to his score, he waddled to the boundary with the ball intact and, on crossing the rope, demanded four runs.

American golfer Bob Goalby was once so disgusted by a shot he'd played that he threw himself into a water hazard.

Trivial Pursuits

There is one subtle difference between Australia's Henley-on-Todd Regatta and England's Henley-on-Thames Regatta – the Todd River is invariably dry. But it's just as well, because all the boats taking part in the Australian event are bottomless. Instead of rowing, the crews poke their legs through the holes in the boats and run along the river bed course.

The World Flounder-Tramping Championships are staged in Scotland's Urr estuary. The flounder – a flat fish – lies on the bottom of the shallow estuary and buries itself in the mud when the tide goes out. Over 200 competitors wade chest-high into the water in bare feet, searching for the tell-tale wriggle of the flounder beneath their toes. The fish can be collected by hand or with a special spear, but must be alive at the weigh-in.

Tobacco-spitting is the name of the game at the annual Calico Tobacco Chewing and Spitting Championships in California. Wads have been ejected distances of over 47ft.

Wales hosts the annual World Bog-Snorkelling Championships. Competitors must swim 60 yards with their snorkels through a dirty, weed-infested peat bog in the fastest possible time. There is rarely a great rush to hug the winner!

Armadillo racing takes place at Fort Worth in Texas.

Every June the Australian city of Darwin stages a Beer Can Regatta in which all the craft are built from beer and soft drinks cans.

Britain's champion gurner was the aptly-named Ron Looney. He won eight national titles.

The tango originated as a dance between two men.

The World Black Pudding Knocking Championships take place at the Corner Pin public house at Ramsbottom, near Manchester. Contestants from as far afield as the US, Australia, Canada and Germany demonstrate their expertise at lobbing Lancashire black puddings on to the roof of the pub in a bid to dislodge the Yorkshire puddings nestling on the ledges. The winner gets his own height in beer.

When crosswords first became popular in the 1920s, two New York magistrates had to ration addicts to a maximum of two puzzles a day after the defendants had been found guilty of neglecting to support their families.

In May 1966 *The Times* heard from a Fijian woman who had just completed the paper's crossword from the edition of 4 April 1932! The woman had been stationed in Fiji as the wife of a civil servant, and that edition of *The Times* had been used to wrap valuables. So it had been untouched for 34 years.

Toy Stories

Since Barbie's creation in 1959, her makers Mattel have bought over 70,000 miles of dress fabric for her wardrobe – enough to stretch from London to Sydney nearly four times.

Barbie sold slowly at first because mothers were reluctant to buy children a doll with breasts.

If Barbie were lifesize, she would have 39-inch breasts.

Sindy's clothes have been designed by such famous names as Mary Quant, Vivienne Westwood and David Emmanuel. The wardrobe designed by Quant caused such a sensation that some of the outfits were sold in children's sizes.

Sindy didn't own a bath until 1972.

Trivial Pursuit took just 45 minutes to conceive.

The yo-yo was based on a Filipino weapon.

There are 1,929,770,126,028,800 possible different colour combinations on a Rubik's Cube.

The Frisbee was modelled on a pie tin made by the Frisbie bakery in Connecticut. The bakery was situated near the University of Yale whose students used to eat the pies at lunchtime and then throw the empty tins to one another.

When two women in south London feared their teddy bear was possessed by an evil spirit, a clergyman was called in to exorcise the demon.

Action Man's US counterpart, G.I. Joe, suffered a hard ride in the wake of the Vietnam War. American toy shops were besieged by protesters bearing banners demanding: "G.I. Joe Must Go."

Colonel Mustard of Cluedo fame undergoes a sex change in Switzerland where he is known as Madame Curry.

Enough rope has been included in Cluedo sets to encircle the world.

Subbuteo took its name from inventor Peter Adolph's favourite bird, the hobby (Latin name: Falco subbuteo subbuteo).

Yo-yos were once banned in Damascus because it was thought they were causing a drought.

When teddy bears first became popular in the 1900s, a US priest denounced them, claiming that they would lead to the destruction of the instincts of motherhood.

More recently a Surrey woman blamed the breakdown of her marriage on the fact that her husband lavished more attention on his 21 teddy bears than he did on her.

Monopoly was initially rejected by games manufacturers Parker Bros for having "52 fundamental playing errors".

In 1983, members of the Buffalo Dive Club played a game of underwater Monopoly. A total of 350 divers played in relays over 45 days.

Rude words are banned from Scrabble in Singapore.

The Name of the Game

Spirograph was invented by electronics engineer Denys Fisher while researching a new design for bomb detonators for NATO.

A 70-year-old tortoise was fitted with a Lego leg. When the creature had to have a front leg amputated after being savaged by a cat, Devon vet John Parkinson replaced the limb with a pair of Lego wheels taken from his son's toy set.

THAT'S ENTERTAINMENT

Poptastic

Charles Manson auditioned unsuccessfully for the Monkees.

Gene Simmons of Kiss has a B.A. and can speak four languages.

Buddy Holly played guitar the wrong way. Instead of strumming up and down, like most guitarists, he played only on the downstroke. So he had to work twice as hard to achieve the sound.

New York band Kid Creole and the Coconuts had seven UK hits between 1981 and 1983, including three in the Top Ten, but never once entered the US Top 100.

At the end of the Beatles song "A Day in the Life", there is an ultrasonic whistle audible only to dogs. This was recorded by Paul McCartney especially for his Shetland sheepdog.

"When Irish Eyes Are Smiling" was written by a German, George Graff, who never set foot in Ireland in his life.

On discovering that his hit "Honky Tonk Angels" was about prostitutes, Cliff Richard demanded that his record company withdraw the single — surely the only instance of an artist banning his own record.

Eddie Cochran's last recording before he was killed in a car crash in 1960 was "Three Steps to Heaven".

Elvis Presley's hip-wiggling started out as stage fright. In the early days he was so nervous on stage that his legs would shake. Since the audience began to scream when he did it, he decided to make it part of the act.

Tommy James was sitting in a New York hotel room looking at the repeated flashing of the Mutual of New York building's neon sign when he had the inspiration for "Mony Mony".

Peter Gabriel played flute on Cat Stevens' "Lady D'Arbanville".

Iggy Pop was born James Jewel Osterburg.

John Denver's real name was Henry John Deutchendorf.

Janis Ian was born Janis Fink.

The Beatles' "Hey Jude" was originally called "Hey Jules". When John Lennon divorced wife Cynthia, Paul McCartney wrote the song to cheer up Lennon's young son Julian.

Chris De Burgh was born in Argentina.

The Singing Nun's 1963 hit "Dominique" was banned by a Massachusetts radio station on the grounds that it was degrading to Catholics.

Romanian folk singer Joan Melu failed to sell a single ticket for her gig at the 2200-seater Capitol Theatre in Melbourne in 1980. Despite the absence of an audience, she proceeded to fulfil her contractual obligation by giving a two-hour performance, complete with interval and encores.

C.W. McCall, who had a hit with "Convoy" in 1976, went on to become mayor of Ouray, Colorado.

American R & B singer Chuck Willis died in 1958 soon after releasing "What Am I Living For?"

John Lennon's first girlfriend was called Thelma Pickles.

Olivia Newton-John's grandfather, Max Born, won the 1954 Nobel Prize for physics.

Luciano Pavarotti received 165 curtain calls and was applauded for an hour and seven minutes by an appreciative German audience.

Sir Tim Rice sang backing vocals on The Scaffold's "Lily the Pink".

As a result of changes to Russian copyright law in 1975, the Rolling Stones became the first rock band to receive Russian royalties.

The Beatles wrote "Dear Prudence" about Mia Farrow's sister, Prudence, when she wouldn't come out and play with Mia and the Beatles at a religious retreat in India.

Twin sisters Kin Narita and Gin Kanie had a hit single in Japan at the age of 99.

Former Monkee Mike Nesmith's mother Bette invented correction fluid.

Unbelievable Facts

As a six-year-old, Ringo Starr nearly died after his appendix burst.

Britain's first disc jockey, Christopher Stone, was the Oxford-educated son of a vicar.

The Rolling Stones' equipment van was dynamited during their 1972 tour of Canada.

David Bowie took his surname from the Bowie knife in honour of his idol, Mick Jagger, a jagger being an old English term for a knife.

The steel drum is the only non-electrical musical instrument invented in the 20th century.

Pat Boone's "Speedy Gonzales" was banned in the US for being offensive to Mexicans.

Madonna's brother Christopher appeared in the video for Soft Cell's "Tainted Love".

Although forever linked with Scotland, the bagpipes were actually first played in Persia hundreds of years ago.

Sheryl Crow's two front teeth are false. The originals fell out when she tripped up on stage early in her career.

David Bowie's former guitarist Mick Ronson is completely deaf in one ear.

That's Entertainment

The 1884 London Telephone Directory included the names of W.S. Gilbert and Sir Arthur Sullivan.

Bruce Springsteen once broke into Elvis Presley's Graceland home in the hope of meeting his idol. But he was caught in the grounds and thrown out.

The lyricist of the song "Keep the Home Fires Burning", Lena Gilbert Ford, died in a fire at her home.

While composing the lyrics for "Yesterday", Paul McCartney used the working words "scrambled eggs" before eventually coming up with "yesterday".

Lynyrd Skynyrd took their name from Leonard Skinner, their school gym teacher who told them: "You boys ain't never gonna amount to nothin'." Leader Ronnie Van Zant decided to keep the name but change the spelling.

Claude Rouget de Lisle composed "The Marseillaise" in return for a bottle of wine. The tune subsequently became the anthem of French Revolutionaries. Ironically, Rouget de Lisle was a royalist who narrowly escaped being guillotined.

In 1968, David Bowie appeared in adverts for the latest rock sensation – the stylophone pocket electric organ.

Both Bing Crosby and Marc Bolan died within weeks of recording TV shows with David Bowie, both dying before the programmes were screened.

The only member of ZZ Top not to have a beard is Frank Beard.

There are something like 50,000 official Elvis impersonators worldwide.

The tune for "The Star Spangled Banner" was written by an Englishman, John Stafford Smith.

In 1996, Clacton resident Sidney Ambrose had to receive medical treatment after clapping too hard at a Beverley Sisters concert.

The BBC took offence at the Kinks' 1970 hit "Lola", not because the lyrics were about a transsexual but because they mentioned Coca-Cola. Ever vigilant about advertising, the Corporation forced Ray Davies to change the words to "Cherry-Cola" when performing on *Top of the Pops*.

In 1971, while Calgary's KFSM radio station was playing Carole King's "I Feel the Earth Move", the studio collapsed.

In Excess

Roky Erickson, singer/guitarist with psychedelic Texan band The Thirteenth Floor Elevators, was convinced that he was an alien from Mars.

Jethro Tull singer Ian Anderson used to walk around with a lampshade on his head.

Sky Saxon, singer with cult Californian band The Seeds, used to live in a dustbin like his hero Top Cat.

Diana Ross used to insist on having cellophane wrapped toilet seats.

Mariah Carey demands that pink toilet rolls be placed in all her hotel rooms. She also refuses to drink from anything but crystal glasses.

Madonna has a tattoo of Marilyn Monroe's face on her bottom.

Donna Summer's birthday cake once travelled first-class on a plane.

Opera singer Enrico Caruso was arrested for pinching a lady's bottom in the monkey house of New York Zoo.

Elvis Presley used to enjoy hanging out at his local morgue and studying the corpses. He was also obsessed by guns and often used his TV set for target practice.

Manfred Mann gave away a mountain to promote his 1974 song "The Good Earth". Everyone who bought the environment-friendly record was rewarded with a deed to a square foot of Welsh mountainside.

Viv Stanshall, zany leader of The Bonzo Dog Doo-Dah Band, once put raw meat into Ringo Starr's drum kit in an attempt to wreck their sound.

When Eric Clapton fell in love with a totem pole during a 1969 tour of the US, he had it flown home and placed in the grounds of his Surrey mansion.

Loretta Lynn got married at 13 and had four children by the time she was 18.

Roy Harper once gave the kiss of life to a sheep.

Arthur Lee, frontman with 1960s band Love, had a tendency to wander off stage during concerts to go to the supermarket.

Before talking to UK MTV, Mariah Carey insisted that puppies and kittens be provided so that she could pet them during the interview.

Keith Moon, wild man drummer with The Who, died in the same London flat (owned by Harry Nilsson) as Mama Cass Elliot of the Mamas and Papas. Elliot choked to death on a sandwich in 1974 and four years later, Moon died from an accidental drug overdose.

Producer Phil Spector once held a gun to singer Leonard Cohen's head in the studio in order to get the performance he desired.

Sam Cooke was shot dead in 1964 after wandering into the wrong motel room after a party. Seeing him in a state of undress, the female occupant felt threatened and gunned him down.

Chicago frontman Terry Kath was killed during a game of Russian roulette in 1978. His last words were: "Don't worry, it's not loaded."

Before They Were Famous

As a boy, David Bowie was a huge fan of Lenny the Lion. His father used to run Lenny's fan club.

That's Entertainment

Cyndi Lauper used to clean dog kennels for a living.

Madonna was sacked from New York fast-food restaurant Dunk' Donuts for squirting jam at a customer.

Tom Jones used to do his courting in a phone box at Pontypridd. Years later, when a new phone box was installed, he arranged for the original to be shipped out to his home in Las Vegas to remind him of the many happy hours he spent in there.

Neil Diamond trained to be a doctor.

Bette Midler used to work as a pineapple chunker at a cannery in Hawaii.

While a student at the London School of Economics, Mick Jagger worked as a relief porter at Bexley Mental Hospital. He was paid £4 10s a week.

Edith Piaf used to earn a living by making wreaths.

Ozzy Osbourne once worked as a labourer at a Birmingham slaughterhouse.

Shirley Bassey used to wrap chamber pots in a Cardiff factory.

In the 1960s, David Soul used to appear as a singer in New York wearing a paper bag over his head. He later got his big break singing in a ski mask on television's The Merv Griffin Show where he was known as "The Covered Man".

Annie Lennox used to work at a fish factory.

Dusty Springfield was sacked from her sales job at Bentalls for fusing the store's entire lighting system.

Joe Cocker was an apprentice fitter with the East Midlands Gas Board. He got by with a little help from his friends.

Spanish crooner Julio Iglesias was a goalkeeper with Real Madrid until his footballing career was ended by a car smash.

Billy Joel was a welterweight boxing champion in his youth.

In 1955, Johnny Mathis was ranked joint 85th in the world for the high jump.

Before leaving school in 1969 and going to Warwick University, Sting took a job as a bus conductor.

George Michael was sacked from his Saturday job at British Home Stores for not wearing a shirt and tie in the stockroom.

American soul singer Bill Withers used to make toilet seats for a living. He worked at a Los Angeles aerospace factory, manufacturing toilet seats for Boeing 747s. Appropriately, one of his biggest hits was "Lean On Me".

Nul Points

In 1974 plotters planning a military coup in Portugal used the playing of the country's Eurovision Song contest entry on radio as the signal for the tanks to move in.

There were 138 la's in Spain's 1968 Eurovision Song Contest winner, "La La La".

Norway's 1980 Eurovision entry was about the construction of a hydro-electric power station. Their 1960 song, "Voi-Voi", was an arrangement of a traditional Lapp reindeer-herding call.

Finland scored *nul points* in 1982 with a little ditty protesting about the building of a nuclear power station.

The Austrians called their 1977 entry "Boom Boom Boomerang" in protest at inane Eurovision song titles.

A diplomatic row erupted in 1987 after BBC presenter Ray Moore jokingly referred to the Turkish group Locomotive as "an ugly crowd".

The 1985 Luxembourg entry, "Children, Kinder, Enfants", had previously been rejected by Germany.

Black Lace, ensured of rock immortality thanks to "Agadoo", came seventh in the 1979 Eurovision with "Mary Ann".

Samantha Janus came tenth in the 1991 Eurovision with "A Message To Your Heart".

In 1978 Jordanian TV refused to show the Israeli Eurovision entry on screen. Instead, while Izhar Cohen sang "A-Bi-Ni-Bi", Jordanian viewers saw nothing more than a bunch of flowers. And when it seemed certain that Israel were going to win, Jordanian TV switched to an American detective series, *Bronk*.

Classical Gas

Beethoven used to pour jugs of iced water over his head to stimulate his brain while composing.

Tchaikovsky was awarded a handsome annual allowance by wealthy widow Nadezhda von Meck . . . on condition that they never met. The widow's reasoning was that she was sure she would be disappointed if ever she met her idol in the flesh.

Composer Jean Baptiste Lully, director of music at the court of Louis XIV, died from an injury sustained while conducting. He inadvertently pierced his foot with the long cane which he was beating on the floor to indicate the tempo. An abscess developed, swiftly followed by gangrene.

By the time he composed his Ninth Symphony, Beethoven was completely deaf.

German composer Robert Schumann said that most of his ideas came from two imaginary companions, Florestan and Eusebius. The pair represented the two sides of Schumann's character. Florestan was the outgoing one; Eusebius was shy and passive. The schizophrenic Schumann also had a phobia about all metal objects – particularly keys.

Mozart never went to school. He started to compose his own music at the age of five and at six, played before the Emperor of Austria. His first compositions were published at seven and a year later, he wrote his first two symphonies.

Mozart once composed a piano piece that required a player to use two hands and a nose to hit the right notes.

A violin contains around 70 separate pieces of wood.

Aware that audiences would only see him side on while he was at the piano, Chopin would sometimes shave only half of his face before a recital.

Screen Legends

The sexy bottom wiggle which became Marilyn Monroe's trademark wasn't done purely for effect. She had weak ankles and bandy legs.

James Cagney never said "you dirty rat" in any of his movies.

Warren Beatty's first job in showbusiness was as a rat-catcher. The National Theater at Washington, DC, had been plagued by rats (one had even bitten an actor) and the cast persuaded the management to employ an official rat-catcher. So 17-year-old Beatty, desperate for any kind of job in the theatre, agreed to patrol the alleyway at night.

Charlie Chaplin once came third in a Charlie Chaplin lookalike competition.

Joyce Grenfell, the archetypal English spinster, was American on both sides of her family.

Sophia Loren's first beauty contest prize included several rolls of wallpaper and a tablecloth with matching napkins.

Gary Cooper turned down the role of Rhett Butler in Gone With The Wind because he was sure it would be a flop.

Unbelievable Facts

Mel Gibson's middle name is Columcille. And John Cleese's middle name is Marwood.

Shirley Temple always had 56 curls in her hair.

That most British of actors David Niven made his film debut as a Mexican in a Hopalong Cassidy movie.

In school, both Tom Cruise and Robin Williams were voted Least Likely to Succeed by their classmates.

Tom Cruise enrolled to become a priest at 14, but dropped out after a year.

Such was the antagonism between Peter Sellers and Orson Welles that when they had to appear together at the gaming table in *Casino Royale*, they acted the scene on different days, each performing to a double.

Claudette Colbert insisted that sets be built around her so that she could make all her entrances with the right side of her face shielded from the camera. Furthermore, she stipulated that any shots of her right profile must be long shots.

Michelle Pfeiffer used to work at the checkout at a grocery store.

Yul Brynner used to be a trapeze artist with a circus in France until he was injured in a fall.

Judy Garland was a descendant of 19th-century US President Ulysses S. Grant.

That's Entertainment

Boris Karloff's real name was William Pratt.

And John Cleese changed his from John Cheese.

"Carry On" star Kenneth Williams was obsessed with his bowels. He suffered from piles and so had a deep mistrust of other people's toilets. Whenever he moved into a theatre for a play, he always insisted on having his own personal toilet, for his sole use. Similarly, any visitors to his London flat were never allowed to use the toilet there – they had to go to nearby Tottenham Court Road tube station.

Donald O'Connor made six films with Francis the Talking Mule in the 1950s but handed over his leading role to Mickey Rooney when he learned that the mule was receiving more fan mail than him.

Airplane and *Naked Gun* star Leslie Nielsen is legally deaf.

Jack Palance was shot down in a plane during World War Two. He sustained severe facial burns which needed major plastic surgery.

Fatty Arbuckle got his break due to a blocked drain. A plumber's mate, he was summoned to unblock producer Mack Sennett's pipes one day in 1913 and was immediately signed up as one of the Keystone Cops.

Oliver Reed had an eagle tattooed on his penis.

After graduating from high school, Danny DeVito went to work in his sister's hair salon where he was known as "Mr Danny".

Unbelievable Facts

W.C. Fields was a terrible insomniac. Sometimes the only way he could get to sleep was under a beach umbrella while being sprinkled with a garden hose.

The anagram of Alicia Silverstone is "evil lass in erotica".

James Mason turned down the chance to star in *Botany Bay* because he didn't want to have to stand in a trench for his scenes with the diminutive Alan Ladd.

Jane Seymour was born with one green eye and one brown eye.

During the making of *Cleopatra*, Liz Taylor's then husband Eddie Fisher was paid $1500 a day to make sure she got to work on time.

Clint Eastwood is allergic to horses.

Before breaking into movies, Sylvester Stallone once had a job as a lion cage cleaner.

Mexican romantic lead Ramon Novarro ordered his house guests to wear nothing but black, white or silver so that they blended in with the black and silver decor of his mansion.

When Ava Gardner died in 1990, she left her pet corgi Morgan a monthly salary plus his own limo and maid.

Before appearing as a teenage prostitute in the 1976 film *Taxi Driver*, 13-year-old Jodie Foster had to undergo psychiatric evaluation to make sure that she was capable of handling such a potentially traumatic role.

That's Entertainment

Demi Moore was born cross-eyed.

As a teenager, Ryan O'Neal boxed in Golden Gloves contests.

Silent film star Clara Bow felt so threatened by the arrival of talking pictures that she viewed the microphone as her sworn enemy. On more than one occasion, she was seen to grab the microphone and viciously assault it.

Johnny Depp has a phobia about clowns.

Rex Harrison had a glass eye.

For added realism in the 1988 film *Vampire's Kiss*, Nicholas Cage ate six live cockroaches.

Marlon Brando used to wander so much on his way to kindergarten that his older sister Jocelyn used to take him to school on a leash.

Lupe Velez, star of the American Spitfire series of the 1940s, could rotate her left breast while the other remained stationary.

Ronald Reagan's hearing was damaged for life when a fellow actor let off a gun next to his ear on set.

Richard Harris appeared as King Arthur in *Camelot* with a piece of Elastoplast visible on his neck.

Humphrey Bogart got his scarred lip as the result of being hit on the mouth by the manacled hands of a prisoner he was transporting during the First World War.

Unbelievable Facts

The first Tarzan of all, actor Elmo Lincoln, lived up to the role. When he was suddenly attacked by a lion in the 1918 movie *Tarzan of the Apes*, he snatched a knife from one of the crew and stabbed his feline co-star to death. Ironically, the lion was the only real animal in the film. All the apes were played by American footballers in hairy costumes.

Chesty Morgan, star of *Deadly Weapons*, had a 73-inch chest.

Marilyn Monroe used to bleach her pubic hair.

Candice Bergen is the daughter of ventriloquist Edgar Bergen. When she was small, her father's famous dummy, Charlie McCarthy, had a bigger bedroom and more clothes than her.

Child actor Bobby Driscoll, who played Jim Hawkins in the 1950 version of *Treasure Island*, served time 11 years later for possessing drugs.

Silent movie star Harold Lloyd lost part of his hand while fooling around with what he thought was a fake prop bomb. It wasn't.

Maurice Chevalier's contract with Paramount, signed as talkies were being introduced, was rendered invalid if he ever lost his French accent.

How's this for a pushy stage mum? The mother of child actor Allen Clayton Hoskins dressed him up as a girl to audition for the role of Farina in the Our Gang comedy films of the 1920s. The deception fooled producer Hal Roach, enabling Master Hoskins to appear in drag for two films in the series.

Ten years after being nominated for an Oscar for his role in *Kramer vs Kramer*, former child star Justin Henry was working as a painter and decorator.

The voice coming from Lauren Bacall's lips during the singing scenes in the 1944 film *To Have and Have Not* is that of Andy Williams. As Bacall has such a deep speaking voice, no suitable female singer could be found. So the producers hired Williams instead.

In his early films, Bing Crosby had his prominent ears stuck back with a special gum. But when he became famous, he stopped bothering.

As a child, Ann-Margret's family were so poor that they had to live in an Illinois funeral parlour. Every night she slept next to a casket.

Katharine Hepburn had a phobia about dirty hair. When she was with Twentieth Century Fox, she used to tour the set sniffing people's hair to make sure that it had been washed.

Mel Blanc, who provided the voice for Bugs Bunny, was allergic to carrots.

Actress Natalie Wood suffered from hydrophobia, a fear of water. She drowned in 1981.

Shirley Temple received 135,000 presents on her eighth birthday. She was a millionaire by the time she was ten.

When Cary Grant played the son of Jessie Royce Landis in *North by Northwest*, he was 55 and she was 54.

Unbelievable Facts

Andy Garcia was a Siamese twin. When he was born, he had a twin the size of a small ball attached to his left shoulder. It was surgically removed and died, but Garcia still bears the scar.

Boss-eyed silent star Ben Turpin was insured for $100,000 against the possibility of his eyes ever becoming normal again.

Sean Connery was paid just £15,000 for his first Bond film, *Dr No*.

Dustin Hoffman commanded a mere $17,000 for *The Graduate* in 1967, but two years later he was paid $425,000 for the turkey *John and Mary*.

The father of 1930s American actress Evelyn Venable had a clause inserted in her contract that she was not allowed to be kissed on screen.

Keanu Reeves was born in the Lebanon. Keanu means "cool breeze over the mountains" in Hawaiian.

Charles Bronson had a decidedly non-macho start to life. His family were so poor that he had to wear his sister's old dresses to school.

In *Little Big Man*, Dustin Hoffman's character aged from 17 to 121. Hoffman himself was 33 at the time.

Young Sidney Poitier was sacked from his job parking cars . . . because he couldn't drive. He got first gear muddled up with reverse and ploughed into another car.

That's Entertainment

Sandra Bullock, Bill Cosby and Bruce Willis all used to work as bartenders.

When horror star Bela Lugosi died, he was buried in Dracula's cloak.

Sean Connery was 58 and Dustin Hoffman 51 when they played father and son in *Family Business*.

Keanu Reeves was voted Most Valuable Player in his high school's ice hockey team. He played in goal where he earned the nickname "The Wall".

Burt Lancaster used to sell lingerie at a Chicago department store.

Rock Hudson (real name Roy Scherer) took his name from a combination of the Rock of Gibraltar and the Hudson River.

Mickey Mouse was originally called Mortimer Mouse. Walt Disney got the idea for the character from watching mice play one night in the garage where he was working.

One of Errol Flynn's first jobs was castrating sheep in Australia. He had to bite off the sheep's testicles with his teeth.

Before making it in Hollywood, Alan Ladd ran his own hot dog stand.

Anthony Newley, James Booth, Terence Stamp and Laurence Harvey all turned down Michael Caine's role in *Alfie*.

Unbelievable Facts

Mickey Mouse received 800,000 fan letters in 1933.

Clark Gable is listed on his birth certificate as a girl.

Movie Clips

Erich von Stroheim used real hookers to play prostitutes in his 1927 movie *The Wedding March*.

The name for Oz in *The Wizard of Oz* was thought up when the creator, Frank Baum, looked at his filing cabinet and saw A-N and O-Z.

Some of the chariot racers in *Ben Hur* wore wristwatches.

Hitler was a big fan of Sherlock Holmes. When the Allies reached his bunker in 1945, the two films they found were both Sherlock Holmes movies.

In Samuel Fuller's 1980 war film, *Big Red One*, all of the Nazi concentration camp guards were played by Jews.

A colossal 187,000 people were involved in the making of the Nazi epic *Kolberg*, including units of soldiers recalled from the front. Ultimately the film was seen by fewer people than had appeared in it.

It cost around $200 million to make *Titanic*. In today's terms, it would cost only $123 million to build the ship.

The actor originally chosen to play the Tin Man in *The Wizard of Oz* nearly died because the make-up made him sick. So the producers changed the make-up and changed the actor.

To conserve metal during the Second World War, the Oscars were made of wood.

Luke Skywalker's surname in *Star Wars* was changed at the last minute from Starkiller because it sounded too violent.

The Jack Nicholson film *As Good As It Gets* is known in China as *Mr Cat Poop*.

There are over 13,000 cinema screens in India. Every day more than 15 million Indians go to the movies.

George Lucas was planning to be a racing driver until he suffered a near-fatal crash two days before he graduated from high school. After that, he chose the safer option of movie producer instead.

The extras hired to play convicts in the 1932 film *Hell's Highway* were all genuine ex-cons.

In the 1926 version of *Don Juan*, John Barrymore plants 191 kisses on various women – an average of one every 53 seconds.

American newspaper tycoon William Randolph Hearst specified that all of his newspapers had to mention the name of his mistress and acting protégée, Marion Davies, at least once in every issue.

Tyre tracks can be spotted on the ground in the classic western *Stagecoach*.

TV aerials can be seen on the roofs of Victorian London in the 1966 comedy *The Wrong Box*.

The people of Hong Kong were so alarmed by the prospect of films that the first cinema audiences there had to be paid to attend.

Ronald Reagan's chimpanzee co-star in *Bedtime for Bonzo* died the day before the film's premiere.

Before making his 1934 epic *Cleopatra*, Cecil B. DeMille sent a team on a $100,000 trip to Egypt to study the colour of the Pyramids. The film was in black and white.

The 1968 Czech film *Happy End* runs backwards.

The Vatican newspaper translates Donald Duck as Donald Anus.

MGM once had the menstrual cycles of the company's actresses plotted on a wall chart so that movies could be planned around them.

A scene for the Charlie Chaplin film *City Lights* required 342 takes.

Although Walt Disney had a moustache, none of his employees was allowed to grow one.

During a scene in *The Sound of Music*, an orange-box is clearly visible stamped with the words "Produce of Israel". But the film was set in 1938 – ten years before Israel was founded.

Alfred Hitchcock didn't have a belly button. It was eliminated when he was sewn up after surgery.

The Unkindest Cuts

Mickey Mouse was banned in Romania in 1935 because the authorities thought that the sight of a 10 ft high rodent on screen was likely to scare the nation's children.

Donald Duck comics were once banned in Finland because he doesn't wear pants.

Belgium is the only country that has never imposed censorship for adult films.

Karate films were banned in Iraq in 1979.

So strict was censorship in the United States in the 1930s that British producer Herbert Wilcox found he could only get *Nell Gwyn* released in the US by shooting a special scene, solely for America, in which Charles II married the orange-girl.

No films showing bikinis were allowed on Malta's screens before 1964.

In 1964 the Peking Cinema Institute banned an educational film entitled *Elementary Safety in Swimming in Rivers, Lakes and Seas*. The safety element was considered a bourgeois trait, calculated to undermine revolutionary daring.

Nudity didn't reach the Chinese screen until 1985 when a girl was seen naked in *The Rickshaw Boy*. But even then she was viewed from the rear only.

Until 1977, Indians were not allowed to kiss one another on screen. Kissing in an Indian film was only permissible if one of the lovers was a foreigner.

Unbelievable Facts

Cleopatra was banned in Egypt for 15 years because its star, Elizabeth Taylor, had converted to Judaism.

At the outbreak of the Second World War, the neutral Irish Republic banned all war footage from newsreels.

The film *Paris, Texas* was banned in the city of Paris, Texas, shortly after its release.

In early Clarabelle Cow cartoons, the cow's udder was always discreetly covered by an apron.

All Robin Hood films were banned in Indiana during the early 1950s because robbing the rich to give to the poor was considered to be a trait of communism.

The Mexican censor cut over half an hour from the movie *Silkwood*, removing all the scenes in which Cher was depicted as a lesbian.

The James Dean film *Rebel Without a Cause* was initially banned in Britain and Spain for fear that it would incite violence among young people.

The silent classic *Birth of a Nation*, released in 1915, was banned in the state of Maryland 37 years later for being "morally bad and crime-inciting".

The Germans considered *Casablanca* to be a propaganda film and refused to let it be shown in German cinemas during World War Two. Even after the war, the film was only able to be screened in Germany in a censored version in which all references to Nazis had been removed.

Strange as it may seem, Hitler was very keen on family values. During his years of power, he stipulated that any woman character in a German film who broke up a marriage must die before the closing credits.

A number of the more passionate scenes between Barbara Bates and Danny Kaye in the 1949 film *The Inspector General* were cut on the orders of Kaye's wife.

As Seen On TV
A youthful Tom Selleck appeared twice on *The Dating Game* (the US forerunner of *Blind Date*) but didn't get picked either time.

At the end of an interview with Duran Duran on *The Tube*, Paula Yates realized that she had been sitting on the microphone. So nobody had heard a word.

William Shatner – *Star Trek's* Captain Kirk – claims that a UFO once saved his life after his motorbike had broken down in the desert.

At its peak, the worldwide audience of *Baywatch* exceeded the world population of Muslims.

American mobsters refused to watch the TV series *The Untouchables* because they thought it showed them in an unfavourable light.

What do *Bullseye's* Jim Bowen and composer Franz Schubert have in common? Both were schoolteachers.

Outspoken talk-show host James Whale is a former Surrey Junior Archery Champion.

A *Generation Game* contestant required to fillet fish and open a bottle of champagne had a wooden leg, and a hook for his right hand.

Tom and Jerry were condemned in the 1970s for their "mindless violence".

On a live edition of *Top of the Pops* in 1964, Alan "Fluff" Freeman introduced the Sounds Orchestral hit "Cast Your Fate to the Wind" as "Cast Your Wind to the Fate".

American singer P.J. Proby once appeared on *Top of the Pops* with his arm in a sling after being bitten by his dog.

Former *Bonanza* star Lorne Greene had one of his nipples bitten off by an alligator while he hosted the TV series *Lorne Greene's Wild Kingdom*.

Singer Adam Ant played a hired killer in *The Equalizer*.

Sonny and Cher played a dress cutter and a model respectively in *The Man From U.N.C.L.E.*

Janet Street-Porter trained to be an architect.

Comedienne Pat Coombs needed 28 takes for a TV advert for muesli because she kept forgetting the name of the product.

George Reeves – TV Superman of the 1950s – shot himself dead in 1959.

Robson Green's middle name is Golightly.

Before changing his name to Engelbert Humperdinck, Gerry Dorsey was turned down by *Opportunity Knocks.*

One in four Americans have appeared on TV.

Convicts on a chain-gang in America's Deep South threatened to riot when a warden said he'd stop them watching *The Fugitive.*

Cliff Richard was accused of "crude exhibitionism" and of being a bad influence on teenagers when he appeared in the 1950s pop show *Oh Boy!*

Patrick McGoohan rejected an offer to play The Saint because he didn't approve of Simon Templar having a new girlfriend each week. It didn't bother Roger Moore.

Boy George paid £42,000 to play himself as a kidnap victim in an episode of *The A-Team.*

George Michael turned down the chance to play a waiter in *Miami Vice.*

Michelle Collins started her career as one of Mari Wilson's backing singers.

For a 1950s BBC production of *Robin Hood*, the back-projection plate was inserted incorrectly so that the trees in Sherwood Forest appeared on screen upside-down.

Unbelievable Facts

Bob Wilson's middle name is Primrose.

While filming his role as King Harold in the 1970s series *Churchill's People*, Dennis Waterman suffered an eye injury courtesy of the lace of his cloak.

Militant students in Prague postponed a rally to watch the sixties drama *The Forsyte Saga*.

Loyd Grossman was singer/guitarist with Jet Bronx and the Forbidden who got to number 49 in 1977 with "Ain't Doin' Nothin'".

As leather-clad Cathy Gale in *The Avengers*, Honor Blackman once knocked out wrestler Jackie Pallo during rehearsals.

The famous dum-de-dum-dum theme from *Dragnet* was actually composed by Miklos Rozsa for the 1946 film noir classic *The Killers*.

Patrick Moore accidentally swallowed a fly during a live transmission of *The Sky at Night*.

Dale Winton was named after Dale Robertson, tough-guy hero of westerns *Tales of Wells Fargo* and *Iron Horse*.

Oprah Winfrey should have been called Orpah after the Biblical figure. But the midwife spelt the name wrongly on the birth certificate.

In the original *Randall & Hopkirk (Deceased)*, Kenneth Cope, who played Marty Hopkirk, wore his wig the wrong way round for two episodes before anyone noticed.

Emma Freud was once a backing singer for Mike Oldfield.

A misheard instruction to the *Top of the Pops* crew meant that Dexy's Midnight Runners performed their 1982 soul tribute "Jackie Wilson Said" in front of a huge blow-up of darts player Jocky Wilson.

Funny Business

The working title for *Last of the Summer Wine* was *The Library Mob*. It was originally intended to set the series in back-to-back terraced houses in Rotherham.

Marcel the monkey was sacked from *Friends* because of his unfortunate tendency to vomit live worms on set.

The 1978 ITV sit-com *Life Begins At Forty*, starring Derek Nimmo and Rosemary Leach, was sold to East Germany — not as comedy, but as part of an adult education initiative to increase the country's birth rate.

Liz Taylor made a voice-only appearance on *The Simpsons* by gurgling baby Maggie Simpson's first words.

Matt Le Blanc, Art Garfunkel and Harrison Ford all once worked as carpenters.

Vic Reeves was once accused of attacking a photographer with a tin of rice pudding.

The American network banned the words "breasts" and "virgin" from *M*A*S*H*. Writer Larry Gelbart overcame the ban by inventing a soldier from the Virgin Islands.

Dick Van Dyke and his TV wife Mary Tyler Moore always had to sleep in separate beds on *The Dick Van Dyke Show* in case they upset moral watchdogs.

Curiously, the first American sit-com couple to be seen regularly sharing a bed were Herman and Lily Munster!

TV stations in Port Arthur, Texas, and Lima, Ohio, refused to screen a January 1996 episode of *Friends* because it featured a lesbian wedding.

Eric Sykes was sacked from his job at a Lancashire cotton mill for singing "In the Blue of the Night" with a bucket on his head.

Michael Crawford (real name Michael Dumble-Smith) took his stage name from a passing Crawford's biscuit lorry.

Bill Cosby was once offered a trial with the Green Bay Packers American Football team.

Miss Piggy was banned from Turkish TV during religious festivals so that viewers wouldn't be offended by the sight of an "unclean" animal.

Jamie Farr (cross-dressing Corporal Klinger in *M*A*S*H*) was the only member of the cast to have served as a soldier in the actual Korean War.

Appearing in a convent play at the age of four, Dave Allen accidentally exposed himself to the nuns when the zip in his frog costume burst. As he hopped about, the nuns tried to drag him off stage.

Alexei Sayle once worked as a school "dinner lady".

Des O'Connor used to play football for Northampton Town. He was a lively winger.

Angus Deayton had trials with Crystal Palace.

Jerry Seinfeld used to have a job selling light bulbs.

Ellen DeGeneres once sold vacuum cleaners for a living.

The success of *Black Adder* was no laughing matter for 70-year-old Mrs. Florence Blackadder of Sheffield. For years she received phone calls from people asking to speak to her husband, the dastardly Blackadder. She begged him to change their name by deed poll.

The role of Frasier was originally offered to John Lithgow.

Andrew Sachs needed hospital treatment while playing Manuel in *Fawlty Towers*. For the scene where he had to run from the blazing kitchen, his jacket smoking, special chemicals were put on his clothes to produce the desired effect. But the chemicals seeped through to his skin and burned his arm. He had to have the burns dressed daily for three weeks.

The *Steptoe and Son* horse Hercules died in a 1970 episode but recovered for the 1972 film.

Soap Bubbles

American network ABC refused to allow a fully-dressed Jeff Colby to kiss wife Fallon's foot in *The Colbys* for fear of encouraging foot-fetishists.

In the sixties, Clive Hornby – *Emmerdale*'s Jack Sugden – was a member of Liverpool band the Dennisons who had hits with "Be My Girl" and "Walkin' the Dog".

Elaine Paige once appeared in *Crossroads*.

Before making his name in *The Clockwork Orange*, Malcolm McDowell played PR man Crispin Ryder in *Crossroads*.

Former US President Gerald Ford and Secretary of State Henry Kissinger both guested on *Dynasty*.

Future Monkee Davy Jones played Ena Sharples' grandson Colin Lomax in one episode of *Coronation Street* back in 1961. He wasn't the only pop star on the show in the early sixties – Peter Noone (later of Herman's Hermits) played Len Fairclough's son Stanley.

In an early episode of *Coronation Street* Ena Sharples said she didn't like chocolate eclairs. Eight years later, she ate two on the show and the letters poured in.

Vince Earl – *Brookside*'s Ron Dixon – was a member of Rory Storm and the Hurricanes when they shared a bill with the Beatles in Hamburg. In fact the Beatles were support act to Rory Storm.

Clive James once appeared as a postman on *Neighbours*.

Michael Palin made a cameo appearance as a surfer on *Home and Away*.

Rudolf Hess was a big fan of *Dynasty*.

Are You Sitting Comfortably?

Daredevil presenter John Noakes was once knocked out on *Blue Peter* by a 5 lb imitation marrow. The accident occurred during a demonstration of marrow-dangling. Noakes was taken to hospital for X-rays.

After breaking his ankle in a fall, actor Conrad Phillips, who played Swiss folk hero William Tell in the 1958 swashbuckler *The Adventures of William Tell*, had to play an entire episode from a wheelchair.

In 1966, the BBC tried to postpone an episode of *Pinky and Perky*, entitled "You Too Can Be a Prime Minister", until after the forthcoming general election. The BBC was afraid the programme might contain political bias. In the end there was such a furore that it was reinstated.

At the height of their fame, Pinky and Perky received almost as much fan mail as the Beatles.

When *The Magic Roundabout* was taken off air in 1968, the fiercest petition for its return came from an army camp.

Thunderbirds creator Gerry Anderson created his first sound-proof studio by nailing 1500 empty egg boxes to the walls of a Slough warehouse.

The Beatles were once support act to Lenny the Lion.

Immediately before presenting *Rainbow*, Geoffrey Hayes had a running role as DC Scatliff in the hard-hitting police drama *Z Cars*.

Unbelievable Facts

The flashing lights on the Daleks in *Dr Who* originally came from the indicators of an old Morris car.

While filming *Skippy*, actress Liza Goddard was weed on by a wombat and got lice from an emu. She had to wash in DDT.

Tommy Rettig, Lassie's young human co-star, was sentenced to five and a half years in a US federal prison in 1976 for smuggling cocaine from Peru.

TV dog trainer Barbara Woodhouse once stormed off in a huff after being squirted by Sooty's water pistol.

Sooty was accused of pushing hard drugs in the 1980s following an episode where he shut Sweep in a tranquilizing booth. He was also charged with introducing sex into children's television when Soo his panda girlfriend was introduced in 1964, and of being anti-police after a storybook showed him attempting to hit PC Nab with a hammer.

Clayton Moore, alias the Lone Ranger, used to open supermarkets at $2500 a time. He charged more if he took along Silver.

Postman Pat is seen as a Mafia figure in Japan. Pat has only three fingers on each hand, and the missing little finger is the sign of Japan's Mafia — the Yakuza — who have the finger amputated to show that they have strength of character and can be trusted. The unlikely connection came to light in 1994 when producers tried to sell *Postman Pat* to Japan.

There were over 100 Hammy Hamsters on *Tales of the Riverbank*.

Schoolboy Jimmy Page (later of Led Zeppelin fame) once appeared as a budding guitarist on the fifties children's show *All Your Own*.

Blue Peter was censured in 1964 over a ginger-pop recipe described by the Temperance Union as "a dangerously alcoholic brew".

Roy Rogers was so devoted to Trigger that when the horse died, he had it stuffed and mounted.

Stage Whispers

Lord Lytton's play, *The Lady of Lyons*, opened and closed at London's Shaftesbury Theatre on 26 December 1888. After waiting for an hour, the audience were sent home because nobody could raise the safety curtain.

At the Edinburgh Festival Fringe in 1981, the Bodgan Club performed *2001* in the back of a Hillman Avenger car at various venues around the city. The maximum audience for each performance was four. However the "theatre" ran into trouble with safety officers because the car had neither exit lights nor space between the aisles.

The Smallest Theatre in the World was built on a 650cc motorcycle by Marcel Steiner in 1972. Steiner once performed *The Tempest* in the car park of the Royal Shakespeare Company at Stratford while the RSC was doing a slightly grander version of the same play inside.

Orson Welles regularly wore a false nose on stage because he hated his own.

The curse of *Macbeth* struck during a production in Dublin in 1954. First there was an attempted suicide, then the company manager broke both his legs and finally an electrician electrocuted himself.

Shakespeare has no living descendants.

Norwegian playwright Henrik Ibsen used to keep a pet scorpion on his desk for inspiration.

All productions of *King Lear* were banned in Britain between 1788 and 1820. The government deemed the play inappropriate in view of George III's insanity.

Samuel Beckett's play *Breath* is the shortest performed play ever written. It consists of 35 seconds of human cries and breaths.

Nancy Seabrooke understudied the part of Mrs Boyle in *The Mousetrap* for 15 years and 6240 performances. In all that time, she only got to perform the role on 72 occasions.

The Moving Picture Mime Show's 1985 production at the Edinburgh Festival Fringe was *The Complete Berk* in which actors attached peas to their ears with sellotape. Unfortunately the show had to be cancelled when one performer got a pea irretrievably stuck in his ear.

The Flying Karamazov Brothers from the US did an act where they juggled a fish, a squid and two live kittens. Alas, British audiences were robbed of a chance to see this spectacle at the Edinburgh Festival Fringe when quarantine laws prevented the Brothers from bringing the kittens into the country.

Actor David Raven played Major Metcalfe in *The Mousetrap* for 4575 performances between 1957 and 1968.

Irish comic David McSavage was arrested at the 1998 Edinburgh Festival for threatening to set his genitals on fire during his outdoor show on the Royal Mile.

Spanish playwright Lope de Vega Carpio claimed to have written 100 of his plays in less than a day each. In all, he wrote nearly 2000 plays and 1500 poems.

Write On

In a 1631 edition of the Bible, the word "not" was accidentally omitted from the Seventh Commandment, thus encouraging readers to commit adultery.

If at first you don't succeed . . . Author John Creasey received 768 rejection letters before his first book was published. He went on to write nearly 600 mystery novels.

As an 18-year-old, Lord Archer had a holiday job as a deckchair attendant in his native Weston-super-Mare.

The first book on plastic surgery was written as early as 1597.

Oxford University Press received back a set of page proofs for a book in 1984. They had been sent out for correction 35 years previously.

All officers in the US Confederate army were given copies of *Les Miserables* by Victor Hugo to carry with them at all times.

In his lifetime, Charles Dickens earned no more money from his novels than he did from his lectures.

Sherlock Holmes creator Sir Arthur Conan Doyle was no mean cricketer. He played for the M.C.C. and once bowled the legendary W.G. Grace.

Charles Dickens always slept facing north because he thought it improved his writing.

The Hitch-Hiker's Guide to the Galaxy has been translated into Croatian.

Joe Shuster and Jerry Siegel sold all rights to comic-strip character Superman to their publishers for $65 apiece in 1938.

The Book of Esther in the Bible is the only book which doesn't mention God by name.

Dame Barbara Cartland is a descendant of Robert the Bruce.

Lewis Carroll wrote most of his books standing up.

A translation of the New Testament from Coptic into Latin, published in 1716, remained in print for 191 years. During that time, it sold an average of one copy every 20 weeks.

The first full novel was written by a woman. In 1007 Murasaki Shikibu, a Japanese noblewoman, wrote *The Story of Genji*, a tale of a prince looking for love and wisdom.

That's Entertainment

In 1857, Alfred, Lord Tennyson, Queen Victoria's Poet Laureate, earned less than her official rat-catcher.

Alfred, Lord Tennyson kept a pony named Fanny which used to pull Tennyson's wife along in a wheelchair.

French novelist Marcel Proust kept a pet swordfish.

Lord Byron kept a pet bear at Cambridge University because dogs weren't allowed.

Gone With the Wind was Margaret Mitchell's only book.

The character Scarlett O'Hara in *Gone With the Wind* was originally called Pansy O'Hara.

Centuries before the artist formerly known as Prince became known by a symbol, English poets such as Cynewulf signed their work in the same way.

Cinderella's slippers were originally made out of fur. The story was changed in the 17th century by a translator.

Iceland publishes more books per head than any other country in the world.

George Bernard Shaw lost his virginity to an elderly widow at the age of 29. He was so horrified by the experience that he steered clear of sex for the next 15 years.

Before Johannes Gutenberg started up his printing press in 1454, there were about 30,000 books in Europe.

Unbelievable Facts

Russian writer Konstantin Mikhailov used 325 pseudonyms.

Mary Shelley wrote *Frankenstein* when she was 19.

Dr Samuel Johnson wrote his story *Rasselas* in a single week to pay for his mother's funeral.

Baroness Orczy, author of *The Scarlet Pimpernel*, couldn't speak English until she was 15.

Baroness Orczy based Sir Percy Blakeney (aka the Scarlet Pimpernel) on a man she spotted on the London Underground.

Lord Byron made his half-sister pregnant.

Now regarded as a master of the English language, Polish-born novelist Joseph Conrad couldn't speak a word of English until he was 19.

Mrs. Beeton – the Delia Smith of her day – died in 1865 at the age of 29.

In 1939, Ernest Vincent Wright published his novel *Gadsby*. Although there were over 50,000 words, none contained the letter "e". The only "e"s in the entire book were those in the author's name.

Alice Pollock of Haslemere in Surrey had her first book, *Portrait of My Victorian Youth*, published when she was 102.

Mark Twain's *The Adventures of Tom Sawyer* was the first novel written on a typewriter.

Robert Burns had a pet ewe called Poor Mallie. He even wrote two poems about her.

Although famed for his erotic novels, D.H. Lawrence was a prude and would only make love in the dark.

In 1650 the Bishop of Winchester borrowed a book from Somerset County Records office. It was finally returned to Somerset County Library in 1985, by which time it had accrued a fine of £3000. The title? *The Book of Fines.*

The first cookery book appeared back in AD 62. Published by the Roman Apicius, it described the favourite feasts of the Emperor Claudius.

It's Only Words

After William the Conqueror invaded England in 1066, English wasn't spoken again at court until the 14th century.

The word "dunce" is taken from the name of a brilliant scholar. Duns Scotus – named after his birthplace of Duns in Scotland – challenged the Church's ideas in the 13th century. But his innovative thoughts were rejected by other scholars after his death. They condemned his teaching as stupid, thus changing the meaning of "dunce".

In old English time, a moment was about 90 seconds. A jiffy still is an actual unit of time. It's one-hundredth of a second.

"Stewardesses" and "reverberated" are the longest words that can be typed with only the left hand.

The only 15-letter word that can be spelled without repeating a letter is "uncopyrightable".

The only ten-letter word you can spell using just the top row of letters of a keyboard is "typewriter".

"Eleven plus two" is an anagram of "twelve plus one".

The only five words in the English language where the vowels are in the right order are "abstemious", "abstentious", "arsenious", "arteriosus" and "facetious".

The letter O is the oldest letter. It hasn't changed in shape since its introduction around 1300BC.

Of all the words in the English language, "set" has the most definitions.

The phrase "rule of thumb" is derived from an old English law which stated that a man couldn't beat his wife with anything wider than his thumb.

The term "Dutch courage" dates from the bubonic plague in the 17th century. To avoid contamination, the city of London was sealed off and therefore no food was getting in. The only people prepared to trade with London were the Dutch who used to sail up the Thames, leave food supplies on jetties and take the money which had been left there. Before landing on Britain's plague-infested shores, the sailors used to steel their nerves with liquor – hence Dutch courage. The Dutch were later rewarded with the freedom of the Thames – a concession they still hold to this day.

The word "babe" was in use as far back as 1915.

"Hair of the dog" stems from the medieval belief that if you were bitten by a mad dog you should take one of its hairs and lay it across the wound to heal it. So the best way to cure a hangover is to have another drink — "the hair of the dog that bit you".

A "white elephant" dates back to the ancient kings of Siam who wanted to punish courtiers without actually appearing to do so. Their ploy was to give the offender a rare albino elephant, knowing that it was an offer which dare not be refused. The poor man was therefore left with something he didn't want and couldn't afford to keep.

The dot over the letter "i" is called a tittle.

The most common name in the world is Mohammed.

If you were to spell out numbers, you would have to go to 1000 before you found the letter "a".

"Bimbo" was slang for a prostitute in the 1920s.

Until 1600, "i" and "j" represented the same letter in the English language. So did "u" and "v".

No word in the English language rhymes with "month", "orange", "silver" or "purple".

The word "assassin" derives from "hashishin" because the original Assassins — a fanatical 11th-century Moslem sect — conducted their attacks under the influence of drugs.

The Cambodian alphabet has 74 letters. By contrast, the alphabet of Rotokas, Papua New Guinea, has only 11 letters – a, b, e, g, i, k, o, p, r, t and u.

The language of Taki, spoken in parts of French Guinea, has only 340 words.

The Hawaiian alphabet has 12 letters.

There's no single word to say "yes" or "no" in Japanese.

The Maori name for a hill on New Zealand's North Island runs to 85 letters.

The Scottish word "tartle" is remarkably succinct. It means "to hesitate in recognizing a person or thing, as happens when you are introduced to someone whose name you cannot recall."

Art For Art's Sake

Vincent van Gogh sold only one painting in his lifetime – Red Vineyard at Arles.

Van Gogh once taught languages and maths at a school in Ramsgate.

An unfinished statue by Leonardo was used for archery practice. While he was working in Milan, Leonardo started work on a statue of Francesco Sforza, the father of his patron, Ludovico Sforza. But he never completed the bronze casting. When French soldiers invaded Milan at the end of the 15th century, the bowmen used the unfinished model for target practice. In doing so, they destroyed it.

Leonardo da Vinci's Mona Lisa was originally bought by King Francis I of France to hang in his bathroom.

Paul Gauguin worked as a labourer on the building of the Panama Canal.

French artist Louis Girodet was at his most creative at night. In order to see in the dark, he would light as many as 40 candles on the brim of his hat. He determined his fee according to the number of candles burned while painting the picture.

The painting Whistler's Mother was once bought from a pawn shop.

Van Gogh painted a picture a day for the last 70 days of his life.

Renoir suffered so badly with rheumatism towards the end of his life that he could only paint by strapping the brush to his hand.

If, in a statue of someone on horseback, the horse has both front legs in the air, it means the person concerned died in battle; if the horse has one front leg in the air, the person died as a result of wounds received in battle; if the horse has all four legs on the ground, the person died of natural causes.

Off the coast of Florida, where the sea is only 20 ft deep, stands an underwater statue of Christ. The base of the 9 ft statue rests on the sandy floor and the top is viewed from the surface by tourists in glass-bottomed boats.

In 1961, the Museum of Modern Art in New York displayed Le Bateau, a painting by Matisse. It was 47 days before anyone spotted that it had been hung upside down.

A middle-aged couple from Milwaukee asked an art expert to look at a painting they owned. While he was there, he examined another painting which was hanging on the wall — one which they thought was a Van Gogh reproduction. It turned out to be the original of Still Life With Flowers and sold at auction for $1,400,000.

The Venus de Milo was found by a Greek peasant digging his land.

The equestrian statue of the Roman emperor Marcus Aurelius – the largest bronze Roman sculpture in existence – was once used as a gibbet. In 965, Pope John XIII ordered an unruly city prefect to be hanged from the statue by his hair.

Congo, a chimpanzee at London Zoo in the 1950s, was such a talented artist that Picasso bought one of his paintings.

During one month in 1936, Picasso completed 23 major oil paintings. He produced over 20,000 works in the course of his career.

Ancient Chinese artists freely painted scenes of nudity and sex, but they would never depict a naked female foot.

When Louis François Roubillac began work on his sculpture of composer George Frederick Handel in 1737, he decided he didn't like Handel's own ears. So he modelled the ears on those of a London lady instead.

The artist Raphael was born on 6 April 1483 and died on 6 April 1520.

X-rays of the Mona Lisa reveal that there are three completely different versions of the same subject, all painted by Leonardo, under the final portrait.

Unbelievable Facts

In 1983, a Japanese artist made a copy of the Mona Lisa out of toast.

Leonardo da Vinci was truly ambidextrous. He could paint with one hand and draw with the other at the same time. One of his lesser-known inventions was the stink bomb . . .

ALL CREATURES GREAT AND SMALL

Animal Crackers

Of all the known forms of animal life which have ever inhabited the earth, only around ten per cent still exist today.

For camouflage in the snow, polar bears have been known to cover their black noses with a paw. All polar bears are left-handed.

On average, a hedgehog's heart beats 300 times a minute.

Rats can't vomit.

Tapirs have four toes on each front foot, but only three on each hind foot.

A giant panda can eat nearly 100 lb of bamboo shoots in a single day.

Camels can see with their eyes closed. Their eyelids are transparent from the inside. And they have three eyelids to protect themselves from blowing sand.

A camel can lose up to 30 per cent of its body weight in perspiration and still survive. By contrast, a human would die of heat shock after sweating away a mere 12 per cent of his or her body weight.

Ignore the humps – a camel's backbone is as straight as that of a horse.

The chamois – a breed of mountain goat – can climb 13,000 ft in an hour.

A single colony of black-tailed prairie dogs from Mexico contained around 400 million animals. The area it covered – 24,000 square miles – is almost as big as the Republic of Ireland.

Armadillos always give birth to identical quadruplets. This is because the offspring all come from the same egg which divides during development.

Armadillos are the only animals besides humans that can get leprosy.

Armadillos can walk underwater.

A mole can dig over 80 yards in a single night.

An aardvark's teeth do not grow simultaneously.

Only three per cent of mammal species are monogamous.

Baby shrews are led around in a chain by their mother. Each grips the tail of the shrew in front.

The skin of a polar bear is black.

Llamas greet by gently blowing on each other.

Rats can swim for half a mile without needing to rest.

Many hamsters only blink one eye at a time.

The cells which make up moose antlers are the fastest growing animal cells in nature.

Because of its height, the arteries of a giraffe feature special valves to help pump blood up to its head. Without these valves, a giraffe's heart would have to be as big as its entire body.

Giraffes are the only animals born with horns.

Giraffes have no vocal chords.

Porcupines float in water.

Camel milk doesn't curdle when boiled.

A fully-grown bear can run as fast as a horse.

When the first duck-billed platypus arrived at the British Museum, the curators thought it was a fake and tried to pull its beak off.

The duck-billed platypus can store up to 600 worms in its cheek pouches.

A giraffe has only the same number of bones in its neck as a human.

A kick from a giraffe can kill a lion.

Unbelievable Facts

The reproductive cycle of the rat is so fast that in less than a year two rats can become the progenitors of 15,000 rats.

The backbone of the tiny hero shrew of central Africa is so strong that it can support the weight of a 12 stone man.

An anteater is nearly 6 ft long yet its mouth is only one inch wide.

In order to eat, an anteater sticks its tongue in and out 100 times a minute. It can eat 30,000 ants in one day.

Polar bears can smell humans up to 20 miles away.

Over 99.9 per cent of all animal species that have ever lived on Earth were extinct before the coming of man.

Some species of mice nest in trees. These creatures may go through their entire life without ever setting foot on the ground.

Millions of Scandinavian lemmings march to their death every four years. In the first year of life, reproduction is slow for the little rodent but it gathers pace over the next two years so that by the fourth, the females are almost continually with young. At this point, panic seems to set in. The lemmings fear overcrowding and that there won't be sufficient food to go round. So they abandon their homes and follow ancient migration paths to the sea in the hope of finding more living space. On the way, many drown trying to cross rivers. Others reach the coast but then plunge headlong over the cliffs to their deaths.

All Creatures Great and Small

Ferrets were domesticated over 500 years before cats.

A female lemming can become pregnant when she's just 14 days old.

Baby mink are born blind and can't see until they're a month old. The mating of two mink has been known to last eight hours.

The tiny rock hyrax — a rat-like creature from central Africa — is the closest living relative of the elephant.

A giraffe can clean its ears with its 21-inch tongue. Giraffes and rats can both go without water longer than camels can.

When thirsty, a camel can drink 25 gallons of water in under three minutes.

Guanacos — South American llamas — send messages to each other by raising and lowering their tails.

Skunks can squirt their vile scent over distances of up to 60 ft. But they won't bite and spray at the same time.

A squirrel can fall 100 ft from a tree without hurting itself. This is because it uses its tail as a parachute.

The jerboa, or desert rat, is capable of jumping 45 times its body length, the equivalent of a 6 ft tall man jumping 270 ft.

The desert rat is the ultimate sex machine. It mates up to 122 times an hour.

Male racoons are the only mammals that have an actual bone in their penis.

Every zebra has its own unique pattern of stripes, like a fingerprint.

Thinking its parents were a camel and a leopard, early European explorers called the giraffe a camelopard.

Beavers have been known to build dams up to 2,000 ft long.

Unlike most carnivores, hyena clans are dominated by the females.

The mouth of a hyena is so tough that it can chew a bottle without cutting itself from fragments of broken glass.

A porcupine can swallow considerable quantities of prussic acid and remain none the worse for the experience. The same quantity of the acid would be enough to poison 100 humans.

Sloths move so slowly that algae grow in their hair.

A kinkajou's tail is twice as long as its body. At night it wraps itself up in its tail and uses it as a pillow.

The individual hairs of a chinchilla are so fine that 500 of them equal the thickness of a single human hair.

The Mojave ground squirrel of the United States hibernates for two-thirds of the year.

Since it has no collar-bone, the deer mouse can flatten its body to such an extent that it can squeeze into an opening a quarter of an inch high.

A rodent's teeth never stop growing.

The spines on a new-born hedgehog start to appear within 24 hours.

All the pet hamsters in the world today are descended from a single female wild golden hamster found in Syria in 1930.

Carnivorous animals won't eat another animal that has been killed by lightning.

When warthogs are foraging for food, they shuffle along on their knees so that their flat, sensitive snouts can sniff out underground morsels.

Armadillos can hold their breath for up to six minutes. That's how they are able to poke their noses into the ground in search of insects.

Since it continually loses body heat, a shrew must keep moving to stay warm. If it remains inactive for more than a few hours, it will lose so much body heat that it will freeze to death. So the only time a shrew ever goes to sleep is when it is hibernating.

Rumble in the Jungle
Elephants are the only mammals with four knees and the only ones that can't jump. They also have the longest gestation period of any mammal – 20 months.

During periods of drought, elephants can detect water under-ground.

The average elephant produces 50 lb of dung every day.

A rhinoceros's skin is ten times thicker than human skin.

Elephants walk on tiptoe because the back portion of their foot is all fat and no bone.

A bull elephant will eat 500 lb of foliage in one day and drink around 30 gallons of water.

Despite having a 10 ft-long stomach, a hippopotamus can run faster than a man.

An adult hippopotamus could bite a 12 ft crocodile in half.

A hippopotamus makes 80 per cent of its sounds under water.

A hippo can open its mouth wide enough for a 4 ft-tall child to fit inside.

Hippos have killed more people than any other animal.

A male rhinoceros often remains mounted on a female for over an hour, ejaculating every ten minutes.

A new-born Sumatran rhinoceros is covered with dense, brown hair which gradually thins out as the animal grows.

A rhinoceros's horn is made out of hair.

The very first bomb dropped by the Allies on Berlin during World War Two killed the only elephant in Berlin Zoo.

African elephants have 40,000 muscles in their trunks and are able to pick up one blade of grass at a time.

Monkey Nuts (And Apes)

Proboscis monkeys are the Barry Manilows of the animal world. The nose of some proboscis monkeys hangs seven inches below their mouth.

Chimpanzees have been known to engage in group sex.

Human birth control pills work on gorillas.

Gorillas make a new nest to sleep in every day.

Gorillas are up to eight times stronger than humans. They are strong enough to be able to lift two family cars . . . although nobody has ever seen them try it.

The smallest of all monkeys, marmosets make ultrasonic sounds which humans can't hear.

The scream of a howler monkey can be heard five miles away. So noisy are they that the sound of a family of howlers travelling through the forest has been mistaken for a thunderstorm.

A male baboon can kill a leopard.

A Moo Moo Here . . . Oink, Oink There . . .

A cow produces 200 times more wind a day than a human.

A cow yields nearly 200,000 glasses of milk in a lifetime.

You can lead a cow upstairs, but not downstairs. This is because a cow's knees can't bend properly to enable it to descend a flight of stairs.

Cows have four stomachs.

The Moscow State Circus has a troupe of dancing cows that dance to Russian music and play football.

Bulls don't see red — they're colour-blind.

Horses can sleep standing up.

A pig's orgasm lasts 30 minutes.

Pigs can become alcoholics.

The squeal of a pig often exceeds official noise pollution levels. The average squeal has been measured at between 100 and 115 decibels. Concorde was originally banned from New York's Kennedy Airport because the noise from its engines exceeded 112 decibels at take-off.

A pig's ejaculation can contain as much as a pint of semen.

Pigs, walruses and light-coloured horses are the only animals other than humans which can get sunburn.

By the time they're six months old, pigs will have increased their birth weight by 7000 per cent.

Since piglets grow so quickly, no fewer than 48 little porkers were signed up to play the title role in *Babe*.

In 1984 Priscilla the pig rescued an 11-year-old boy from drowning. Priscilla from Houston, Texas, spotted the youngster struggling to stay above water in Lake Somerville. So she swam to his assistance, used her snout to keep the boy's head above water until he could hold on to her collar, and then dragged him to the safety of the shore.

The placement of its eyes allows a donkey to see all four of its feet at the same time.

A goat's eyes have rectangular pupils.

In 1984, a Canadian farmer began renting advertising space on his cows.

Completely Batty

There are around 1000 species of bat.

Bats have an echo-location system to help pinpoint their prey or any obstacles in their path. When in flight at night, they make rapid squeaks, most of which are too high-pitched for humans to hear. Their ultra-sensitive ears allow them to hear the squeak's echo. Although they fly out of caves in vast numbers, they respond only to their own individual echo-signals and not to those of another bat.

Unbelievable Facts

Bats always turn left when exiting a cave.

Some moths emit jamming signals to confuse bats' high-frequency sound waves.

The china mark moth can tell when a bat is near and quickly falls to the ground to escape its clutches.

A single little brown bat can catch 600 mosquitoes in an hour.

Sometimes bats catch insects in their mouths but they often use their wings like a net to scoop up prey.

Bats aren't blind. Their eyes are small, but work perfectly well.

Vampire bats don't actually suck blood. They bite, then lick up the flow. They drink two tablespoons of blood every day, the equivalent of half their own bodyweight.

Vampire bats can be caring souls. They adopt orphans and have been known to risk their life in order to share food with less fortunate roost-mates.

Whereas most bats prefer insects, the bulldog bat from Central and Southern America is an accomplished fisherman. It trails its extra-long legs in the water and grabs fish with its huge hooked claws.

The bumblebee bat of Thailand weighs less than a small coin.

The great flying foxes of Indonesia have wingspans of nearly 6 ft.

A species of horseshoe bat in India shares a burrow with porcupines.

Woolly bats of West Africa live in spiders' webs.

The tent-building bat of Central America bites into a palm leaf so that it folds down to make a shelter like a tent.

The tube-nosed bat has nostrils which stick out from its nose.

Mexican free-tailed bats fly up to two miles high in order to feed or catch tailwinds.

Migrating bats are sometimes caught up in storms and blown out to sea. Occasionally, they will drop in on ships hundreds of miles from dry land.

Skippy and Co.

Kangaroos and emus can't walk backwards, which is why they feature on the Australian coat of arms.

A kangaroo can't jump unless its tail is touching the ground. The tail provides the necessary leverage for take-off.

Red kangaroos are able to produce simultaneously two different types of milk from adjacent teats.

Baby kangaroos are just an inch long at birth.

Kangaroo rats never drink water. They carry their own water source within them, producing fluids from the food they eat and the air they breathe.

Koala bears don't drink water either. They get fluids from the eucalyptus leaves they eat.

Koala bears sleep for 22 hours a day.

The fingerprints of koala bears are virtually indistinguishable from those of humans.

When opossums are pretending to be dead ("playing possum"), they're not playing. They actually pass out from sheer terror.

Opossums give birth to their young just 12 days after conception.

Kangaroos are superb swimmers and have been found swimming a mile off the shore of Australia.

When baby opossums are born, they are so tiny that an entire litter can fit in a tablespoon.

The male swamp antechinus, a little marsupial from Australia, dies from too much sex. It dedicates its life to non-stop copulation and, unable to find time to feed between romps in the long grass, drops dead from starvation.

Smooth and Slimy

If you weighed all the earthworms in the United States, they would be something like 55 times heavier than the combined weight of all Americans.

A microchaetus earthworm found in the Transvaal in 1937 measured a staggering 22 ft long.

If food is in short supply, a ribbon worm can eat 95 per cent of its own body and still survive.

The female marine worm is thousands of times heavier than her partner. While he is, at most, a puny one-tenth of an inch long, she can grow up to 3 ft in length. There's no doubt who wears the trousers in that house.

Slugs have four noses.

Snails can sleep for three years without waking up.

The sticky discharge that snails produce as they move along a surface forms such a strong protective layer beneath their bodies that they can slide along the edge of a razor blade without cutting themselves.

In 1846, two desert snails were given to the Natural History Museum as dead exhibits. They were glued on a small tablet and put on display. Four years later, museum staff noticed that one of the snails appeared to be still alive and placed it in lukewarm water. It recovered, started feeding and lived for another two years.

Snails kiss before mating. But they only mate once in their life.

A leech has 32 brains.

Paws For Thought

Studies show that if a cat falls off the seventh floor of a building, it has 30 per cent less chance of surviving than one that falls from the 20th floor. This is because it supposedly takes around eight floors for a cat to realize what is happening, relax and correct itself.

Cats have 100 different vocal sounds whereas dogs have only ten.

The domestic cat is the only species of cat able to hold its tail vertically while walking. Wild cats hold their tail horizontally or between their legs when walking.

A cat can't move its jaw sideways.

Cats have a third eyelid, called a haw, which is rarely visible.

All tortoiseshell cats are female except for the occasional sterile male.

The Russian blue cat often has an extra toe.

A four-month-old kitten followed a group of Alpine climbers to the top of the 14,691 ft high Matterhorn in 1950.

Fewer than three per cent of tigers become man-eaters.

Tigers have striped skin, not just striped fur.

Lions are the only cats to live in organized social groups.

No two lions have the same pattern of whiskers.

In 1981 Mehmet Tunc, working in Germany, was on his way back to his native Turkey for a holiday when his cat Minosch disappeared at the Turkish border. A bedraggled Minosch resurfaced 61 days later at the Tunc home on the island of Sylt in northern Germany, having travelled 1500 miles.

Humorist and artist Edward Lear was so devoted to his cat Foss that when he had to move to a new house in Italy, he had it built as an exact replica of the previous abode so that Foss would instantly feel at home.

For centuries the Chinese have used the secretions of the civet in perfume.

Some lions mate more than 50 times a day.

In the wild, a lion usually makes no more than 20 kills a year.

The cheetah is the only cat that can't retract its claws.

In ancient Egypt, people used to shave their eyebrows to mourn the death of their cat. The penalty for killing a cat was death.

Knowing how the Egyptians worshipped cats, the Persians threw dozens of them over the walls of an Egyptian fort they were besieging. Rather than risk injury to the cats in battle, the Egyptians quickly surrendered.

Cats were so precious in Japan that until 1602 they were kept on leads. Then the emperor ordered that they could be released so that they could kill the vermin that were threatening the silk crop.

The first cat imported into Paraguay was sold for 1 lb of solid gold.

Cats cannot taste anything sweet.

There are over 3000 types of domestic cat, but only eight per cent are pedigree.

A cat has 32 muscles in each ear.

A Texan tabby cat named Dusty gave birth to 420 kittens during her life.

In 1953, a Persian cat called Sugar travelled 1500 miles from Anderson, California, to Gage, Oklahoma, after her owners had moved there. They had left the cat with a neighbour in Anderson because the animal had a bad hip. Yet even with her injury, Sugar completed a 14-month trek across the Rockies to meet up with the family again.

In the US, people spend more on cat food than on baby food.

In the rear of a cat's eye is a light-reflecting layer which causes their eyes to glow at night. This layer absorbs light six times more effectively than human eyes do, enabling cats to see better than people at night.

Cats' urine glows in pitch black darkness.

A female tortoiseshell cat named Towser was employed as mouse-catcher by a Scottish distillery. It was estimated that she killed nearly 28,900 mice in her life – an average of three a day.

Cats, camels and giraffes all walk by moving their front and back legs on one side together.

The cat is the only domestic animal not mentioned in the Bible.

No new animals have been truly domesticated in the last 4000 years.

Dog Tales
The basenji hunting dog from Africa can't bark. Instead it makes a peculiar yodelling sound.

Hunting dogs not owned by William the Conqueror had three toes removed to slow them down when trying to catch game.

Dalmatians are born almost pure white. Their spots develop as they get older.

One in ten Dalmatians is born deaf.

Dalmatians are the only dogs that can get gout.

Seven out of ten British dogs get Christmas presents from their owners.

Apart from humans, dogs are the only animals with prostates.

It was once against the law to have a pet dog in parts of Iceland.

Chinese crested dogs can get acne.

In South Wales in 1972, a male dachshund crept up on a sleeping Great Dane bitch. The unlikely union resulted in 13 dogs with short legs and large heads.

Dogs don't sweat by salivating. They sweat through the pads of their feet.

Surveys indicate that Afghan hounds are the most stupid breed of dog.

Before the 1978 act which made it compulsory for dog owners in New York City to clean up after their pets, some 40,000,000 lb of dog mess was deposited on the streets every year.

Every year, London parks are drenched in one million gallons of dog urine.

The bloodhound is the only animal whose evidence is admissible in a US court.

In Spain, poodles were once used to sniff out truffles.

A bull terrier called Billy caught 4000 rats in 17 hours in London in 1825. What makes the feat all the more remarkable is that Billy was blind in one eye.

In a recent survey, a third of dog owners in the United States admitted talking to their dogs on the phone or leaving messages for them on answering machines.

In 1998, Scarborough Football Club awarded club membership to one of their most loyal fans – an eight-year-old lurcher dog called Honey.

Mary Queen of Scots and Charles I were both accompanied to their executions by their faithful dogs.

In 1983, Spot, a cross-bred sheepdog, jumped on board a London-bound National Express coach in Cardiff and refused to move until the vehicle arrived at London's Victoria Coach Station. There Spot jumped off but, half an hour later, just as the coach was about to begin its return journey, he jumped back on, occupied the same seat and completed a 310-mile round trip.

Frederick the Great had an unhealthy interest in his whippet bitches.

Canine movie star Rin Tin Tin had a valet, a personal chef, a limousine and a chauffeur for his own exclusive use. The dog also had his own five-room dressing-room complex on the studio lot.

When Ella Wendel of New York died in 1931, she left £15 million to her standard poodle Toby.

Silent movie star Clara Bow had the fur of her two Chow dogs dyed red to match the colour of her own hair.

Composer Edward Elgar used to take his three dogs for long drives in his open-topped car . . . all wearing goggles.

Dobermans take their name from a German tax collector. Ludwig Dobermann bred the animals to help him put the frighteners on his clients.

Remarkable Reptiles and Amazing Amphibians

Frogs never drink. They absorb water from their surroundings by osmosis.

Although they're reptiles, garter snakes don't lay eggs. They can give birth to as many as 85 babies at a time.

The male garter snake takes no chances with his partner's fidelity. Immediately after mating, he seals up the female's sexual opening with a plug made from kidney secretions. This acts as a chastity belt and keeps her on the reptilian straight and narrow.

The Polynesian skink has a vivid blue tail, deliberately designed to attract predators. When attacked, the skink simply sheds its tail which, thanks to a series of automatic muscle spasms, continues to wriggle around of its own accord. With the predator distracted by the writhing tail, the rest of the skink slips away unnoticed.

The paradoxical frog of South America is smaller as an adult than as a tadpole. Whereas the tadpole can reach a length of 10 in, the adult never exceeds 3 in.

A crocodile can't stick its tongue out.

The tuatara lizard, which lives on islands off the coast of New Zealand, has a third eye. Situated on top of the lizard's head, the eye has no iris and so cannot focus on an image. However it can differentiate between light and dark, helping the tuatara to determine the time of year for giving birth.

Sea turtles can eat poisonous Portuguese man-of-war jellyfish without coming to any harm.

Male turtles grunt, females hiss.

Russian scientists found a salamander which had been frozen in ice for 90 years. It woke up from its long hibernation when they warmed it up.

A chameleon's tongue can be twice as long as its body.

A chameleon can move its eyes in two directions at the same time.

Some lizards have no legs.

Rattlesnakes hibernate in colonies of up to 1000. Remarkably, they share a site with prairie dogs – the rattlesnake's favourite snack when not in a state of hibernation.

When snakes are born with two heads, they fight each other for food.

The deadly black mamba can reach speeds of 12 mph over short distances.

A frog's tongue grows from the front of its mouth.

Toads don't have teeth, but frogs do.

The ears of the male and female American tree frog are tuned differently. While humans can hear the frog's complete call of "coqui", the male frog is only able to hear the first part ("co") and the female can only hear the second part ("qui").

A poison arrow frog has enough venom to kill 2,200 people.

Over 50 per cent of people who go untreated after being bitten by venomous snakes in the United States, still survive.

Snakes have no ears. So they don't hear a snake-charmer's music – they react to his movements and vibrations.

More people per head die from snakebites in Sri Lanka than in any other country in the world. On average, two people are killed there every day.

The most venomous species of snake in the world has never actually killed anyone. The fierce snake has enough venom to kill 250,000 mice but because it lives in the remote Australian outback, it rarely comes into contact with people and has yet to cause a human fatality.

Grass snakes sometimes eat adders.

When toads vomit, they don't only bring up the contents of the stomach but the stomach itself. The stomach hangs from the toad's mouth for a few moments before being re-swallowed.

Toads live at altitudes of over 26,000 ft in the Himalayas.

The horned lizard squirts a thin stream of blood from the corners of its eyes when frightened.

Giant komodo dragons aren't poisonous, but their mouth is so full of germs and disease that a bite can still prove fatal.

A species of gecko from the Caribbean is no more than an inch and a half long.

The female common toad sometimes suffocates under the sheer weight of lovers. Since there is always a shortage of females, the male desperately clings on to her back and may be carried around for several days before the eggs are laid. In the meantime, he has to fend off rival males eager to dislodge him. If a male is dislodged, others frantically climb on to the female, forming towers of up to ten toads. Even if the female does suffocate under this load, the males still hang on for a number of days while her body decomposes beneath them.

Geckos can run upside down across a ceiling because of the ingenious pads on their feet. These pads consist of thousands of fine bristles, covered with even finer hairs which end in Velcro-like hooks. The density of the hairs enables them to act as suction pads and to allow the little lizard to support several times its own weight while hanging upside down.

Some geckos have three tails.

The venom of a baby rattlesnake is lethal as soon as it is born. And a rattlesnake's poison can remain potent for 25 years after its death.

There is a flying snake in Asia. Before launching itself from a tree top, it flattens its body, spreads its ribs and drives out all the air from its lungs. This makes it thin and flat, enabling it to glide through the air. When it wants to change direction, it twists its body.

When attacked, the chuckwalla, a large lizard from the United States, wedges itself into a crack between two rocks and puffs itself up so that it can't be pulled out. It can inflate its lungs to increase its body size by 50 per cent.

A single toad may catch and eat up to 1000 insects in one summer.

A baby ten-inch Nile crocodile will grow to 19 times that length as an adult. If human babies grew at the same rate, the world would be full of 31 ft people.

Crocodiles can't chew. They clamp their prey in their jaws and twist a lump off by writhing around in the water.

So that they don't suffer from indigestion, crocodiles always carry around 5 lb of pebbles in their stomach.

The digestive juices of crocodiles contain so much hydrochloric acid that they have dissolved iron spearheads and six-inch steel hooks that have been swallowed.

A king cobra kept at London Zoo measured a colossal 18 ft 9 in. When war broke out in 1939, zookeepers killed it, afraid that it would escape and pose a danger to Londoners.

Pythons are able to go more than a year without food.

The male Darwin's frog from Chile swallows the eggs his mate lays and keeps them in a sac under his chin. Able to accommodate up to 17 tadpoles, he waits until they are big enough and then opens his mouth and releases them into the outside world.

Some frogs can be frozen solid then thawed, and continue living.

The goliath frog from the African Congo can reach the size of a small terrier.

Common toads unable to find a female in the breeding season will try and mate with just about anything – including sticks, water lilies and goldfish.

Basilisk lizards can move so quickly that they can run across rivers. Their thin, fringed toes barely break the surface of the water while their long tail acts as a rudder.

Australia's shingleback lizard has a fat tail which makes it look as if it's got two heads. This fools hungry birds into attacking the wrong end.

The babies of shingleback lizards are huge – about half the size of their mother.

A lizard that lives in the Namib Desert in Africa keeps cool by balancing on one or two legs and waving the others in the air. When it gets really hot, it lies on its belly with all four feet off the scorching sand.

A pair of Indian pythons were once observed copulating for 180 days.

The axolotl salamander from Mexico is the Peter Pan of the amphibian world – it never grows up. As long as it remains in water (which can be for its entire life), it retains its larval tadpole-like shape. It can even breed in this form. But if forced to live on land, it can adopt the adult form of a salamander with lungs in place of gills.

The prehistoric stegosaurus had a brain the size of a walnut.

Ruff Justice

At Basle, Switzerland, in 1471, a cockerel was found guilty of laying an egg "in defiance of natural law". The bird was burnt at the stake as "a devil in disguise".

At Stelvio in northern Italy, a warrant was issued in 1519 for the arrest of a gang of moles after crops had been severely damaged. The moles were summoned to court and when they failed to appear on the specified date, they were sentenced to exile. In its mercy, the court promised the moles safe conduct, along with "an additional respite of 14 days to all those which are with young."

President Eisenhower hated cats so much that he ordered any trespassing on his land to be shot.

In 1857 an American soldier was found guilty of having sex with a mare. Both parties were sentenced to death. The soldier's sentence was subsequently commuted to exile, but the horse was executed.

A monkey was once tried and convicted for smoking a cigarette in South Bend, Indiana.

A dog was sentenced to life imprisonment for killing an American governor's cat. The dog ended up serving six years.

In 1670 the authorities of Munster banished a plague of fleas from the city, prohibiting them from returning for ten years.

In 1740, a cow in France was hanged after being found guilty of sorcery.

An Alsatian dog was arrested in the Spanish city of Seville in 1983 for snatching handbags from shoppers.

French lawyer Bartholomew Chassenée successfully defended a group of rats which were charged with destroying a barley crop in 1521. When the rats failed to appear in court to answer the charges, Chassenée claimed that his clients had been intimidated by cats belonging to the prosecution. He demanded an undertaking that the cats would not attack the rats on the way to court. When the prosecution refused to guarantee the rats' safety, the case was dismissed.

In New Zealand, a cow was sentenced to two days in prison for eating the grass in front of the city courthouse.

Bizarre Birds

The tail of the quetzal from Central America is so long that it has to take off from a branch by launching itself backwards into space like a parachutist.

Male geese sometimes form homosexual tendencies.

Turkeys are so stupid that in arctic temperatures they will stand and freeze to death rather than walk a few paces to the warmth of their hutches.

Despite its long legs, the secretary bird can't run. Instead it hops along the African scrubland in search of its favourite diet of snakes and lizards. It then stamps its victims to death.

As its tongue is too short for its beak, the toucan must juggle its food before swallowing it.

Ducks only lay eggs early in the morning.

A female pigeon can't lay eggs if she's alone. In order for her ovaries to function, she must be able to see another pigeon or, failing that, her own reflection.

The flamingo always feeds with its beak upside down.

The young hoatzin of the Amazon basin has claws on its wings. It is a throwback to archaeopteryx which lived around 140 million years ago.

The home of the Great Indian hornbill is a prison. When the female is ready to lay her eggs, she hides in a hole in a tree. The male then seals up the hole, leaving just a narrow slit through which he passes food. Safe from predators, the female remains locked up until the chicks are a few months old.

The sooty tern remains continually aloft for as long as ten years before returning to land to breed. Until then, it never lands – eating, drinking and sleeping on the wing.

When eating, vultures often gorge themselves to the point where they can't fly. So to lighten their load and make a quick getaway if threatened, they will regurgitate the meal.

The male bower bird builds and decorates a small hut to attract a female. After building the structure with twigs, he adds colourful objects such as feathers, fruit, shells, pebbles and glass. The atlas bower bird goes as far as painting the walls – by dipping bark or leaves into the blue or dark green saliva he secretes. When finally satisfied with his handiwork, he performs a love dance outside the hut, frequently offering the female a pretty item from his collection in an effort to impress her.

Hummingbirds can only perch. They can't walk or run.

Herring gulls have been known to swoop on golf balls in the mistaken belief that they are shellfish.

Since there is no vegetation in Antarctica for nest building, the male Emperor penguin incubates the egg on its feet for 54 days. The egg is kept warm under a flap of skin below the penguin's belly. During this period, the adult is unable to feed or even move. Penguins ignore any egg which rolls off the nest, but will cheerfully try and incubate jam jars or glasses.

A North American osprey once built a nest made up of three shirts, a bath towel, an arrow and a garden rake.

A nest of the North American redhead – a species of duck – had no fewer than 87 eggs. This was because several ducks had used the same nest instead of building their own.

The wrybill – a New Zealand plover – has a beak that curves sideways. It uses this to probe for insects under stones on beaches.

The turkey vulture squirts excrement on to its legs and feet to stay cool.

The mallee fowl of Australia keeps its eggs warm by burying them in a compost heap of rotting vegetation. During incubation the parents ensure that the temperature inside the compost heap remains at a constant 91°F by adding or removing layers of vegetation as necessary. Ironically, after such parental care and devotion, the moment the chicks are born, they are left to fend for themselves.

The woodcock has eyes set so far back in its head that it has a 36-degree field of vision, enabling it to see all around and even over the top of its head.

Although the kiwi of New Zealand is only about the same size as a chicken, it lays an egg which is ten times larger than a hen's. The kiwi's egg is nearly a quarter of its body weight.

The nostrils of a kiwi are at the end of its long beak.

The kiwi can't fly, lives in a hole in the ground, is nearly blind and lays just one egg a year. Yet in spite of this, it has survived for over 70 million years.

Winged Wonders

The wandering albatross can glide for six days without beating its wings and can even sleep in mid-air while gliding at 35 mph. Its wing span can reach 11 ft – that's about twice the height of Tom Cruise.

Although albatrosses live at sea and are associated with ships, they are invariably seasick when brought on board a vessel.

An ostrich's eye is larger than its brain.

An ostrich egg takes 40 minutes to hard-boil. The shell is so strong that it can support the weight of a 20-stone man.

On its death, an ostrich at London Zoo was found to have swallowed an alarm clock, 3 ft of rope and a quantity of coins.

The Japanese Phoenix fowl has been known to grow tail feathers nearly 35 ft long.

A peregrine falcon can spot a pigeon five miles away.

A duck's quack doesn't echo.

As many as 150 weaver birds join forces to build a communal nest high up in a tree.

An eagle can kill a young deer and fly off with it in its talons.

The longest recorded flight of a chicken is 13 seconds.

Starlings were introduced to the US by a group that wanted to bring to America every species of bird mentioned in Shakespeare's works.

Chickens will lay bigger and stronger eggs if you change the lighting in such a way that they think a day is 28 hours long.

Around 75 per cent of all wild birds die before they are six months old.

The bird with the widest variety of diet is the ruffled grouse from North America. It will tackle at least 518 different kinds of animals and insects and 414 different plants.

Over 10,000 birds a year die from smashing into windows.

An African grey parrot named Prudle retired undefeated after winning best-talking bird prize at London's National Cage and Aviary Bird Show for 12 successive years. She had a vocabulary of nearly 800 words.

The cassowary from Papua New Guinea and Northern Australia is the most dangerous bird in the world. It can kill a person with one kick.

To survive, most birds must eat at least half their own weight in food each day.

Penguins are the only birds that can swim but can't fly.

Penguins can jump 6 ft in the air.

Eagles can have sex while flying at 60 mph. It is not uncommon for both birds to hit the ground before they finish.

Sandgrouse live in deserts and every day fly up to 50 miles to a water-hole to drink. Since the chicks can't fly to reach water, the parents take it to them. They ruffle their belly feathers and soak them in water, then fly back to the nest with the water held in their feathers like a sponge. The chicks then suck the moisture from the feathers.

A puffin can carry as many as ten fish in its beak at a time.

Puffins are the only birds to moult their beaks. With other birds, beaks constantly grow and wear down throughout their lives, but puffins have brightly coloured beaks for the mating season. Afterwards, the outer layer is shed, leaving them with smaller, dull beaks for the rest of the year.

Ninety per cent of all species that have become extinct have been birds.

Whereas each of our eyes takes up about five per cent of our head, a bird's eye occupies around 50 per cent of its head.

The pied flycatcher is a two-timing love rat. The male will often try and pair off with two females, but he likes to keep them over a mile apart so that they don't find out about each other. If both of his females lay eggs and hatch them out, he will then desert one and only feed the chicks of the other.

The bones of a pigeon weigh less than its feathers.

One male sage grouse has been known to mate with as many as 21 females in a morning.

Only male cockatoos can be taught to talk. Similarly, only male canaries sing.

Penguins only have sex twice a year.

Eagles can swoop at over 100 mph, but can brake to a halt in just 20 ft.

Bald eagles aren't bald. The top of their head is covered with slicked-down white feathers and from a distance this makes the birds appear bald.

Crossbills are born with straight beaks so that their parents can feed them easily. The bill only starts to hook over when the chicks are six weeks old.

Some owls have fringes on their primary feathers to enable them to fly in silence. This not only allows them to approach undetected, but it also allows them to hear their prey.

The owl parrot can't fly. It builds its nest under tree roots.

The toucan's huge beak is hollow. It is made from a hard spongy material with large air spaces in it. This makes it strong enough to use but light enough to carry around.

A parrot's beak can close with a force of 350 lb per square inch.

The oilbird spends its entire life in darkness. It lives in the caves of South America, only venturing out at night to feed on fruit. It finds its way around in the caves by echo-location in the same way as a bat.

Canaries can regenerate their brain cells.

The jacana of Africa has the longest toes of any bird – up to three inches long. The elongated toes spread the bird's weight so that it can walk across lily pads in search of food without sinking.

During the First World War, parrots were kept on the Eiffel Tower to warn of approaching aircraft. Due to their acute sense of hearing, they could detect planes long before they came into the range of human lookouts.

The penguin is the only bird that walks upright.

The world's heaviest flying bird is the great bustard which weighs in at around 46 lb – the same weight as a six-year-old boy. By rights, it should be too heavy to fly.

Young gannets are fed so much fish that they can't fly. When they leave the nest, they have to fast for a couple of weeks until they are light enough to get airborne.

There are around 40 separate muscles in a bird's wing.

In China, cormorants are trained to catch and retrieve fish. A light chain is put around each bird's neck to prevent it swallowing the fish it has just caught.

All Creatures Great and Small

The wandering albatross is at its heaviest when it is still a nestling. A baby albatross can weigh up to 35 lb, but it loses weight when it starts to exercise its wings and is about one third lighter by the time it is able to fly properly.

A pair of swifts can catch up to 20,000 insects in a single day.

The tailorbird uses its sharp beak to pierce holes along the edges of leaves. It then makes a nest by stitching the leaves together with blades of grass.

Many owls have one ear bigger than the other and one ear higher than the other. This difference makes it easier for them to judge precisely where a sound is coming from and so pinpoint prey even in pitch darkness.

A woodpecker's tongue reaches right round the inside of its head.

A pelican's pouch can hold three gallons of water – as much as a large bucket. The pouch is so big that it can hold several times more food than the pelican's stomach.

In 1810, the United States passenger pigeon was just about the commonest bird in the world. Over two billion were estimated in a single flock. Yet by 1914 it was extinct.

Starling roosts can contain as many as two million birds.

Owls are the only birds that can see the colour blue.

The owl is also the only bird to drop its upper eyelid in order to wink. All other birds do it by raising their lower eyelid.

Owls have such big eyes that there is no room for them to move in their sockets. Instead they turn their whole head to look sideways. Due to their flexible necks, they can turn their head right round to look backwards.

Whereas eagles can go without food for several days, the tiny goldcrest needs to eat all day long in winter just to have enough energy to survive the nights.

There is one poisonous bird in the world — the pitohui from New Guinea. It has a toxic alkaloid, similar to that of a poison arrow frog, on its feathers and skin.

A baby robin eats 14 ft of earthworms a day.

Robins have a life expectancy of just 18 months. So the same robin that seems to appear in a garden year after year is almost certainly a succession of different birds.

The ground finch of the Galapagos Islands is a vampire. Using its sharp beak, it pecks holes in the wings of nesting masked boobies and drinks their blood.

Hummingbirds can fly backwards. A hummingbird's wings beat 80 times per second.

While awake, hummingbirds must eat at least every half an hour or they will starve to death.

Hummingbirds drink eight times their weight in water each day – the same as a man drinking nearly a bath-full of water.

Although measuring less than an inch long and weighing just one tenth of an ounce, each autumn the ruby-throated hummingbird propels its little body on a non-stop 500-mile flight from the United States across the Gulf of Mexico to South America.

The palm nut vulture of West Africa is a vegetarian bird of prey – the only one in the world. Its main food is the fruit of the oil palm tree, although it has been known to lapse into eating the occasional fish.

Swifts remain airborne for between two and four years at a time. They sleep, drink, eat and even mate on the wing.

It has been estimated that a young swift flies non-stop for over 300,000 miles between leaving the nest and making its first landing.

Flamingos can live for up to 80 years.

Bearded vultures can eat tortoises. They crack open the tortoise's shell by dropping it on to a rock.

Some bee-eaters hitch a ride on the back of storks or bustards so that they can snap up any insects which are disturbed by the larger bird's feet.

Flamingos aren't naturally pink. They get the colour from their food – tiny green algae which turn pink during digestion.

The shrike, or butcher bird, impales its victims — usually mice, lizards or small birds — on sharp thorns while it eats them.

The reed warbler can sing two tunes at once. And the gouldian finch of Australia goes one better. Not only can it sing two tunes simultaneously but for good measure it can throw in a droning sound like a set of bagpipes.

Some Japanese herons have got fishing down to a fine art. They pick up insects, drop them on the surface of the water and when the fish rise to the bait, they are speared by the heron's beak.

The beak of the red-headed woodpecker hits the bark of a tree at 1300 mph — over twice the speed of a bullet. The force is such that, by all known laws of science, the bird's head should fall off.

Hard to Fathom

The climbing perch can leave the water and shin up trees in pursuit of insects.

Dolphins never completely sleep, since the two halves of their brain shut down alternately.

Captive dolphins masturbate regularly, even when females are present.

Dolphins that live in the Amazon are pink.

The ovaries of barnacles are in their heads.

When a school of baby catfish are threatened, their father opens his mouth and the youngsters swim inside to hide until the danger has passed.

A catfish has over 27,000 taste buds.

The deep-sea angler fish has its own special rod, line and bait for catching prey. Living in the dark depths of the Atlantic, it has a bony projection above its mouth. From this stretches a long, thin line like a fishing rod, the end of which is illuminated by bacteria. The angler fish waves the pole about and little fish come to investigate in the belief that the moving light is food.

In some species of angler fish, the smaller male literally hangs on to his partner for life. Their bodily systems become united and he becomes entirely dependent on the female's blood for nutrition.

One in 5000 North Atlantic lobsters is born bright blue.

Some species of bass spend the first five years of their life as females before changing into males.

90 per cent of all lobsters die a week after hatching. And the odds are 10,000 to 1 against any larval lobster living long enough to end up on a dinner table.

The average cod deposits between four and six million eggs at a single spawning.

Cleaner wrasse swim into the mouths of larger fish to take scraps of food stuck in between the teeth. They approach the bigger fish with a wriggling motion which seems to prevent them being eaten.

Unbelievable Facts

A shrimp's heart is in its head.

The tiny hatchet fish of South America emits from its body ghostly, greenish-white lights which, to the uninitiated, resemble a row of ferocious teeth. As a result, predators tend to give it a wide berth.

The deep-sea clam of the North Atlantic takes around 100 years to reach a length of one-third of an inch.

Dead sponges can resist bacterial decay for over five years when submerged in fresh water.

A starfish can turn its stomach inside out. Starfish don't have any brains.

Not all starfish have five arms. The sun starfish has 13 and the feather star has ten.

Clown fish swim in and out of the tentacles of a sea anemone without getting stung. The sea anemone acts as a kind of patron to the clown fish, allowing it to lay its eggs at the base of the anemone's tentacles where they are safe from enemies. The incentive for the anemone is that the presence of the clown fish attracts other fish, eager to attack it. When the predator falls victim to the anemone's sting, the anemone and the clown fish share the resulting meal.

Lobsters have blue blood.

A four-inch long abalone – an edible marine snail – can grip a rock with a force of 400 lb. Two grown men would be unable to move it.

Shrimps can only swim backwards.

The small remora hitches a ride on the body of sharks. Otherwise known as the sucker fish, the remora has a suction pad on its head which enables it to cling to the shark. Once attached, it feeds on small animals that stick to the shark's skin.

When attacked, the sea cucumber throws out sticky threads from its mouth which entangle the enemy. While the aggressor is a bit tied up, the sea cucumber makes its escape.

Minnows have teeth in their throat.

There were once more sea lions on Earth than people.

Unbelievable Facts

The seahorse is the only creature where the male becomes pregnant. When ready to breed, the female releases her eggs into a special pouch in the male's stomach. He then discharges his sperm over them. Once the eggs are fertilized, the male's belly takes on that familiar rounded shape.

A solitary sturgeon once yielded £189,350 worth of caviar.

Fish sometimes suffer from seasickness.

Sticklebacks make a nest of water weeds. If the baby stickle-backs swim away from the nest, the male will chase them, suck them into his mouth and then spit them back into the nest.

Apart from humans, dolphins are the only species which have sex for pleasure.

An adult walrus eats about 3000 clams a day.

A walrus walks on its teeth. It uses its long tusks to pull itself out of the sea and to drag itself along on land.

Flying fish have been known to soar to heights of 20 ft and to stay in the air for distances of over 600 ft. In fact, they glide rather than fly. They rise almost to the water surface and, by rapidly vibrating their tail fin from side to side at 50 beats per second, reach speeds of 34 mph. They then use their pectoral fins as wings and leap into the air, gliding close to the surface where they can flick their tail against the water to gain extra impetus. They can also change direction in mid-flight.

Atlantic salmon can leap 15 ft into the air.

The archer fish can catch insects even when they're out of the water. The fish uses its tongue like a water pistol and fires a "bullet" from a special tube at any unsuspecting insect sitting on a leaf. The insect then topples from the leaf and into the water where it is eagerly devoured. The archer fish can hit insects at distances of over 3 ft above the surface of the water.

In the Caribbean, there are oysters that can climb trees.

A single shoal of herring can stretch for over six miles.

Mexican cave fish don't have any eyes. They spend their entire lives in dark underwater caves.

When they are young, flatfish such as plaice or sole have eyes on both sides of their head, like conventional fish. But after a few weeks, one eye starts to move across the top of the head to the other side. The fish then lie flat on the ocean bed with both eyes on the upper side of their body. In the event of danger, they quickly conceal themselves by covering their body in sand, leaving only their eyes showing.

Pistol shrimps stun their prey by emitting shock waves from their pincers.

The mudskipper of the tropical African swamps leaves water to catch insects on land. To get out of the water, it curls its tail against the mud and jerks its body straight. It can walk or hop on land for bursts of a few minutes at a time because, although it has no lungs to enable it to breathe in air, it keeps its gill chamber full of oxygenated water.

The sea hedgehog, or globefish, often swims upside down.

Oysters change sex depending on the temperature of the water around them.

Robber crabs can climb trees. Wrapping their legs around tree trunks, they shin up trees in search of coconuts.

Tuna never stop moving. They swim at a steady rate of 9 mph for their entire lives. Scientists estimate that a 15-year-old tuna will have travelled in the region of one million miles.

A limpet moves from its rock to look for food when the tide comes in and returns to precisely the same spot when the tide goes out again.

If you keep a goldfish in a darkened room, it will eventually turn white. A pregnant goldfish is called a twit.

Goldfish can see both infra-red and ultraviolet light – the only creatures to be able to do so.

A goldfish has a memory span of three seconds. That long?

Until 1938, when a fisherman caught one in the Indian Ocean, the coelacanth was thought to have died out 60 million years ago.

The Columbus crab doesn't have a shell of its own. So it lives on debris washed up on the shore. If its body is ever exposed to the sun, it dies immediately.

A pet goldfish which died in England in 1980 was an amazing 41 years old.

Monsters of the Deep

A giant squid's eyes are larger than a human head, as much as 18 in across. Yet its eyesight is much worse than a human's.

Humans eat more sharks than sharks eat humans.

Barracuda are more likely to attack humans than sharks are.

Barracuda can be dangerous even when dead. If they're feeling ill, they eat all manner of rubbish, making their flesh extremely poisonous to eat.

A whale's penis is called a dork and can extend up to 10 ft. But it is the humble barnacle which has the largest penis of any animal in the world in relation to its size. The male barnacle is able to extend it to the nearest female on his chosen rock.

Some of the biggest whales – including the humpback, blue and minke – don't have any teeth.

A blue whale's heart beats just nine times per minute.

Since a whale's eyeball is fixed, it must move its entire body to shift its line of vision.

A sperm whale's brain is six and a half times larger than a human brain.

Unbelievable Facts

A blue whale weighs 90 million times more than a pygmy shrew.

A blue whale eats five tons of krill, which are tiny crustaceans, every day.

Electric eels can produce a discharge of 650 volts – enough to stun a small horse. Their power to shock is so great that they can overcome victims from 15 ft.

Unlike most fish, electric eels can swim both backwards and forwards. They don't get enough oxygen from the water and so every five minutes they must come to the surface to breathe.

Some species of eel lay up to 20 million eggs. Then the female dies.

A jellyfish is 95 per cent water. Even when dead, a jellyfish can sting.

Jellyfish can't swim. They are carried along by the wind and by water currents.

The sting from the Australian sea wasp, or box jellyfish, can kill a human in four minutes.

Spread out, the tentacles of the Arctic giant jellyfish would form a circle across an area bigger than 15 tennis courts.

The pain threshold of a shark is so high that nothing seems to deter them. Sharks eating rapaciously have been known to continue feeding even after other sharks have attacked and half eaten them. A shark will also eat parts of its own body that have become detached.

Of over 250 species of shark, only 18 are known to be dangerous to humans.

Scientific research indicates that sharks are the only creatures not to suffer any form of illness. They are thought to be immune to every known disease, including cancer.

A large shark can bite through steel cables. Sharks' teeth are constantly renewed. Teeth at the front of the mouth are replaced by new teeth at the back in a kind of conveyor-belt process. Large sharks have up to 1000 teeth.

A shark can detect one part of blood in 100 million parts of water. The good news is that the chances of being attacked by a shark are 30,000,000 to 1.

Items found inside sharks' stomachs include torpedoes, bicycle parts, crates of drink, car number plates, a horse's head, a porcupine, bottles of wine, petrol cans and even a suit of armour.

Although sharks have gills, they can't pump water over them like other fish. So they have to keep swimming in order to push water over their gills. Consequently sharks never stop swimming — even when they're asleep. If they did, they would drown.

The embryos of tiger sharks fight each other inside the mother's womb. Only the survivor is actually born.

There have been examples of an octopus removing stings from captured jellyfish and attaching them to its own tentacles as an added weapon.

Whales can communicate with each other over a distance of 700 miles.

Fully-grown whales eat three tons of food a day.

Piranhas can strip a fully-grown alligator of all its flesh in five minutes. During an attack, they race each other to be first to finish off the corpse.

Piranha teeth are so sharp that Amazonian natives use them as scissors.

In 1981 over 300 people were eaten alive by piranhas when a ferry capsized as it was docking at the Brazilian port of Obidos. There were only 128 survivors.

Percy the piranha, a monster specimen who lived at a Morecambe marine centre, was electrocuted when he bit through the heating cable in his tank.

Squid move by jet propulsion. By forcing water through flaps along its body, the squid can move equally fast backwards or forwards.

When it's born, a baby blue whale weighs approximately the same as a fully-grown hippopotamus.

A species of giant clam found on the coast of Malaysia is strong enough to be able to drown a human being. It grows to a width of more than 3 ft and can weigh over 440 lb. If a swimmer were to get his foot caught in the clam's mouth, he wouldn't be able to pull it out again, and would eventually drown.

Squid and octopuses have three hearts.

The giant spider crab of Japan measures 12 ft wide from the tips of its claws. If it felt so inclined, it could hug a hippopotamus.

If an octopus becomes unduly stressed, it may eat itself.

Insect Asides

Since the female bedbug has no sexual opening, the male drills a vagina, using his penis as a drill. He then inserts his sperm into the female.

The larva of the polyphemus moth of North America eats the equivalent of 86,000 times its own birth weight in the first two months of its life.

Scorpions can withstand 200 times as much radiation as a human can.

An ant can lift 50 times its own weight, pull 30 times its own weight, and always falls on its right side when intoxicated.

A rhinoceros beetle can support 850 times its own weight on its back.

Mosquitoes are responsible for more deaths worldwide than any other creature.

In one "sitting", a mosquito can absorb one and a half times its own weight in blood.

Only female mosquitoes bite and drink blood.

Mosquitoes prefer blondes to brunettes.

Mosquitoes are attracted to the colour blue twice as much as any other colour.

One species of cicada spends the first 17 years of its life asleep underground as a nymph. Then it wakes up, emerges as a fully-grown winged cicada and dies just five weeks later.

A housefly hums in middle octave, to the key of F.

Insects have yellow blood.

Stick insects have been known to have sex for 79 days at a time.

The water-boatman swims on its back on the water surface, rowing along with its rear legs.

Bees have five eyes. They have two large compound eyes (one either side of their head) and three primitive eyes on top of their head to detect light intensity.

To warm their wings up for flight, bees often bask in the sun for a few moments before taking off.

When threatened, the caterpillar of the elephant hawk moth retracts its legs and rolls over to display a pair of false "eyes", just like those of a deadly pit viper. Not surprisingly, the predator tends to give it a wide berth.

All Creatures Great and Small

Cockroaches can live for over a week with their heads cut off . . . but will eventually die of starvation.

The world's termites outweigh the world's humans by ten to one.

A swarm of locusts which swept across Nebraska in 1874 covered an estimated 198,600 square miles. There were thought to be around 12.5 trillion insects in the swarm, although no one was counting.

Even small swarms of locusts can weigh thousands of tons.

The caterpillar of the king page butterfly camouflages itself as bird droppings.

Grasshoppers can only hop if their body temperature exceeds 62°F.

A grasshopper can leap over obstacles 500 times its own height.

Tree ants produce their own glue. When the adult ants build a nest of leaves, they squeeze a sticky substance from the bodies of the young grubs and this gums the edges of the leaves together.

When ants find food, they lay down a chemical trail so that other ants can find their way from the nest to the food source.

Ants stretch when they wake up in the morning.

Unbelievable Facts

The leaf-cutting ants of South America grow their own food. They forage for plants and leaves which they carry home. Then they chew the pieces into a form of compost which they spread on the floors of their underground chambers. Eventually fungus grows on the compost and is eaten by the ants.

A fly can react to something it sees and change direction in 30 milliseconds.

A housefly can transport germs up to 15 miles from the original source of contamination.

The average house fly lives for just two weeks.

Caterpillars have three times as many muscles as humans do.

Only female honeybees can sting. The males are harmless.

Male bees die after mating with the queen bee. Their penises break off.

The male moth mite is born as a mature insect. As his newborn sisters emerge from the mother's sexual cavity, he immediately grabs them with his hind legs and mates with them. While he is waiting for more unsuspecting sisters to be born, he drills a hole into the side of his mother's body and feeds on her juices.

Insects consume ten per cent of the world's food supply every year.

A dragonfly can reach speeds of 25 mph.

Centipedes sometimes have as few as 28 legs. And millipedes never have 1000 legs – usually more like 80.

The male tick doesn't have a penis so instead he pokes around the female's vagina with his nose. When her opening is large enough, he turns around and deposits sperm from his rear on to the entrance of her orifice. He then uses his nose to push the sperm deeper into the vagina.

The silkworm moth has 11 brains.

A typical bed houses over six million dust mites.

Earwigs got their name because it was widely believed that they liked to burrow into human ears.

The necophorus beetle is nature's undertaker. When a small animal dies, the stench attracts the male beetle which proceeds to push the corpse to a suitable burial spot. Using some of the animal's fur as a nest, the female beetle then lays her eggs in a tunnel leading from the burial chamber. When the eggs hatch, the grubs feed on the meat from the scavenged body.

Scorpions are not immune to their own poison.

Over 306 million ants were found in a single colony in Japan. There were 45,000 connecting nests built over an area of one square mile.

The ant has the largest brain in proportion to its size of any living creature.

Crickets hear through their knees, their hearing organs being situated on the front legs.

Tests suggest that the best time to spray household insects is 4 pm. Apparently that's when they're at the most vulnerable.

In a beehive, only 1½ oz of wax are used to build a comb that will hold 4 lb of honey.

Each year, bees kill more people than venomous snakes.

When the bombardier beetle is startled, it squirts a spray from glands in its rear. The repellent spray stops the enemy in its tracks long enough for the beetle to make its escape.

The average life of the mayfly is less than five hours.

If you weighed all the world's insects against all the other animals on the planet, the insects would be heavier.

Insects outnumber humans by 100 million to one.

Scientists discover up to 10,000 new species of insect every year. And it's thought that there are anything between one million and ten million species still undiscovered.

If you put a drop of alcohol on a scorpion, it will immediately go mad and sting itself to death.

Butterflies can't fly if their body temperature drops below 86°F.

Butterflies taste with their feet.

All Creatures Great and Small

A monarch butterfly's sense of taste is 12,000 times more refined than that of a human.

Termite queens are fertilized regularly by the same mate for life – unlike bee and ant queens whose male partners die after the first and only mating.

The Japanese beetle of the United States and Canada can chew through a human eardrum in a matter of minutes.

An ant can survive for two weeks underwater.

The egg of the Malaysian stick insect is bigger than a peanut. At half an inch long, the egg is one-twelfth of the entire body size of the insect.

The female praying mantis eats her partner after sex . . . and sometimes even during sex. The female is much larger than the male and during copulation hooks her deadly arms around him and starts to nibble away. His sex drive is so strong that he can carry on even while being eaten.

An insect exerts so much energy in one hour of flying that it may lose one-third of its overall body weight.

In flight, a midge beats its wings over 1000 times a second.

The male gypsy moth can "smell" the virgin female gypsy moth from 1.8 miles away.

Some crickets burrow special tunnels which help transmit the sound of their chirrups to a distance of 2000 ft.

Unbelievable Facts

Queen termites can live for as long as 50 years. During that period they lay an egg every second.

There are at least 850,000 different kinds of insects in the world.

The caterpillar of the monarch butterfly multiplies its birth weight by 2700 times. If a 7 lb human baby gained weight at the same rate, as an adult it would weigh over nine tons.

A flea can jump as high as 8 in – 130 times its body size. This is the equivalent of a human jumping almost 350 ft in the air.

Fleas are essential to the health of hedgehogs because they stimulate the animal's skin. A deloused hedgehog will die.

Bees can see ultraviolet light.

Bombyx mori, a silkworm moth, has been cultivated for so many years that it can no longer exist without human care. As it has been domesticated, it has lost the ability to fly.

Fireflies like to light up together. Two fireflies near each other will light up at the same time.

Ladybirds can eat 100 aphids a day.

A cockroach's favourite food is the glue on the back of postage stamps.

Cockroaches can travel at over 3 mph – the equivalent of 50 body lengths per second.

Cockroaches have lived on Earth for 250 million years without changing in any way.

Honeybees communicate with each other by a complicated system of round-dancing and tail-waggling. But they have different dialects. For example, Italian honeybees cannot understand Austrian honeybees. The Italian changes from the round to the waggle when food is about 115 ft from the colony whereas the Austrian does so at 260 ft.

Water mites are big on bondage. During mating, the male pins the female to the ground with tiny hooks so that there is no escape. He also glues himself to her with a special secretion. And the legs of the male sometimes double as sex organs.

The glow from six large fireflies provides sufficient light for reading a book.

The male scorpion fly camps it up to get attention. By pretending to be female, he persuades the other males to bring him food.

In one year, a single cabbage aphid can give birth to offspring weighing over three times the total weight of the world's human population. Luckily, most don't survive.

The Worldwide Web
A spider's blood is transparent.

A species of spider in India spins webs with strands that are more than 20 ft long.

Unbelievable Facts

No two spider webs are the same.

In relation to its size, a common house spider can run eight times faster than an Olympic sprinter.

There is a spider in Western Samoa that is no bigger than a full stop.

After mating, the female black widow spider devours her partner. She may eat as many as 25 mates in a day.

The venom of a female black widow spider is more potent than a rattlesnake's.

In return for him narrating a documentary, the US Natural History Museum named a spider after Harrison Ford – *Calponia Harrisonfordi*.

The strands of a spider's web are as strong as steel of the same thickness.

The water spider lives underwater and breathes by trapping a bubble of air in its body.

Some baby spiders in Australia bite limbs off their mother and feed on them over a period of weeks.

A goliath bird-eating spider found in Venezuela in 1965 had a leg span the size of a dinner-plate.

On average, a person swallows three spiders a year.

Armed Shrubbery

The grapple tree of South Africa produces a fearsome fruit called the "Devil's Claw". The fruit is covered in lethal hooks which latch on to passing animals. As the animal tries to shake the fruit off, the hooks embed themselves deeper in the flesh. If the animal touches the fruit with its mouth, the fruit will attach itself to the animal's jaw, inflicting enormous pain and preventing it from eating. Whilst antelope are the usual victims, lions have also starved to death as a result of an encounter with the Devil's Claw.

The bladderwort floats on the water's surface. When an insect gets too close, the special bladders on the plant's leaves open and water is sucked in, along with the unfortunate insect.

The leaves of the pitcher plant of Malaysia are shaped to form a pitcher. These can be as much as 20 in deep and are a deadly trap for insects and even small animals such as rats and frogs. The victims are lured inside the pitcher by its brightly-coloured rim and nectar-secreting walls. But once inside, they fall foul of the slippery, waxy surface and slide to a slow, painful death in the lethal cocktail of rainwater and digestive acids which gather at the bottom of the pitcher.

It takes another carnivorous plant, the Venus fly trap, half an hour to squash and kill a fly and ten days to digest it.

Although carnivorous plants are partial to a nice piece of steak, cheese gives them indigestion.

Potty Plants

The rare *Puya raimondii* of Bolivia can take up to 150 years to bloom. And as soon as it has done so, it dies.

The giant rafflesia of Borneo and Sumatra is a parasitic plant which attracts carrion-loving insects by looking and smelling like a lump of rotting meat.

Seeds of the lotus plant have been known to germinate 3000 years after being dispersed.

The roots of some Finnish pine trees can extend for 30 miles.

The Lady in the Veil mushroom from tropical Africa is one of the fastest-growing organisms in the plant world. It takes a mere 20 minutes to attain its full height of eight inches. To achieve this, its cells expand at such a rate that they make an audible cracking sound.

A single orchid plant was sold in 1952 for $4500.

An orange tree brought to France in 1421 lived and bore fruit for 473 years.

Mistletoe was used by ancient Druids in their sacrifices. They also prepared it as a drink for curing sterility and as a protection against poison.

The 6 ft wide leaves of the Amazon water lily are strong enough to support the weight of a child.

Giant sequoia trees and redwoods can live for 6000 years. A redwood which fell in California in 1977 was believed to be at least 6200 years old.

The trunk of a giant sequoia growing in California is over 102 ft round. The tree is 275 ft tall and it is estimated that it contains enough timber to make five billion matches.

The bark of the redwood tree is fireproof. Fires in redwood forests take place inside the trees.

If a raindrop or an animal hits the giant puffball fungus, thousands of spores are puffed out of a hole in the top. In a single day, a giant puffball can release as many as seven billion spores.

The banyan tree produces rope-like shoots from its vast spreading branches that take root to form new trunks. A 200-year-old specimen in Calcutta Botanic Gardens has over 1775 trunks. During Alexander the Great's Indian campaign, as many as 20,000 soldiers are said to have sheltered under a single banyan tree.

The onion is a member of the lily family.

When the fruit of the South American sandbox tree is ripe, it explodes with such force that the seeds can be scattered nearly 50 ft from the main trunk. The explosion is so loud that those experiencing it for the first time often mistake it for gunfire.

The world's smallest species of tree is a dwarf willow which grows to just two inches in height on the tundra of Greenland.

A eucalyptus growing in Australia in the 19th century stood over 500 ft tall.

During an average growing season, a mature oak tree gives off 28,000 gallons of moisture.

Acorns are poisonous to humans and can cause kidney damage if eaten.

Oak trees don't produce acorns until they're at least 50 years old.

The baobab tree of Africa and Australia stores over 35,000 gallons of water in its trunk to make it drought-resistant.

The blossoms of the baobab tree open only in moonlight.

The saguaro cactus of the Arizona Desert grows less than an inch in its first ten years.

A single ragweed plant can release as many as one billion grains of pollen.

If touched, the aptly-named sensitive plant of Brazil collapses in one-tenth of a second. This deters predators and, within ten minutes, once the danger has passed, the plant returns to its upright position.

The centre of the titan arum grows three inches in a day. The flowers last for a single day and give off a stench of rotting flesh, which is why in its native Sumatra it's known as the "corpse flower".

The sausage tree has long fruits which look just like sausages. However the Ashanti people of Ghana call the tree "nufatene' which means "hanging breasts", comparing the fruit to old tribeswomen whose life of breastfeeding results in elongated breasts.

It takes 400 crocuses to produce a single ounce of saffron.

Some bamboos can grow 34 inches per day.

Some mushrooms glow in the dark and are visible from distances of up to 50 ft. Consequently they are sometimes used as lanterns in remote jungle regions.

The number of trees felled in one day around the world would cover the island of Barbados.

Research at the University of Sussex has shown that plants grow faster to music. Their favourite turned out to be Meat Loaf's "Bat Out of Hell".

FOOD AND DRINK

Fruit and Veg

Women used to rub crushed strawberries on their breasts in the belief that it would make them bigger (the breasts, not the strawberries).

The strawberry is technically not a fruit at all. Botanically speaking, fruits are seed-bearing structures which grow from a flower's ovaries. The strawberry is merely the swollen base of the strawberry flower – the plant's true fruits are the small, nut-like pips embedded on the outside of the flesh.

The loganberry is named after an American judge. Californian Judge J.H. Logan was a keen fruit-grower who crossed a wild blackberry with a cultivated raspberry and came up with his own fruit.

Lemons contain more sugar than strawberries.

Most of the vitamin C in fruits is in the skin.

Apples are more efficient than caffeine for waking you up in the morning.

The first frozen food on sale in Britain was asparagus.

Rejected potato crisp flavours include strawberry fool, mince pie and apricot.

Unbelievable Facts

The belief that spinach makes you strong is based on a printing error. In 1870, a misplaced decimal point in a set of published food tables made spinach appear to contain ten times more iron than other vegetables. In fact, it has much the same iron content. It's a good job nobody told Popeye.

Raw broccoli contains twice as much vitamin C as an orange.

Broccoli is a vegetable with a nervous system. Experts believe that it *can* feel pain.

Caroline of Brunswick, wife of George IV, used to ride around with a pumpkin on her head to keep cool. From George's description of her, it probably improved her looks as well . . .

Over a third of the world's commercial supply of pineapples comes from Hawaii.

The most valuable nutrients of a potato are in the skin.

Potatoes belong to the same family as deadly nightshade.

The Jerusalem artichoke is a native of North America.

Research shows that mosquitoes are particularly attracted to people who have recently eaten bananas.

During the Second World War, American pilots in the Pacific were given asparagus as part of their emergency rations. This wasn't to add a taste of *haute cuisine* to their diet, but to help them catch fish. The idea was that any pilot who found himself stranded on a desert island should eat the asparagus and then urinate into the sea. The strong chemical attractants in the asparagus would pass into the urine and lure the fish.

The ancient Egyptians believed that mixing half an onion with beer foam would ward off death.

Until 1830 tomatoes were thought to be poisonous.

Tomatoes were also thought to be powerful aphrodisiacs. The tomato became known as the "love apple" because the English thought the French called it *pomme d'amour* ("apple of love"). But in fact the French called it *pomme du Moor* because it had come to Europe via North Africa.

A potato has no more calories than an apple.

It takes more calories to eat a stick of celery than the celery itself has in it.

The ancient Greeks awarded celery to their sporting champions.

The custom of serving a slice of lemon with fish dates back to the Middle Ages. It was thought if a person accidentally swallowed a fish bone, the lemon juice would dissolve it.

Apple pips contain cyanide.

More than 7000 varieties of apple are grown in the world.

The only vegetables that aren't annuals are asparagus and rhubarb.

When potatoes were first introduced to Europe in the 17th

century, they were blamed for outbreaks of leprosy and syphilis. As late as 1720 in the United States, eating potatoes was believed to shorten a person's life.

Food for Thought
Chocolate contains the same chemical – phenylethylamine – that your brain produces when you fall in love.

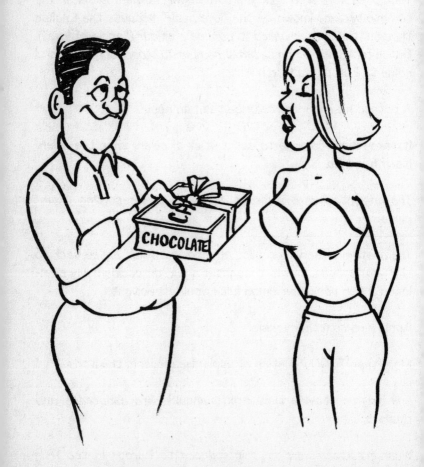

Food and Drink

During your lifetime, you'll eat around 60,000 lb of food – the weight of six elephants.

Rice is the principal food for half of the world's people. The world's daily helping of rice would make a pile as big as Egypt's Great Pyramid.

There are over 15,000 different kinds of rice. The Chinese alone eat 530,000 tons of rice every day.

Half of the foods eaten in the world today were developed by farmers in the Andes – including potatoes, chocolate, maize, peanuts, tomatoes, peppers and strawberries.

There are an average of 178 sesame seeds on a McDonald's Big Mac bun.

The favourite pizza topping in Australia is eggs. In Chile, it's mussels and clams.

The Pilgrim Fathers refused to eat lobster because they thought it was a big insect.

Lobster was so common in 18th-century Maine that it was used for fertilizer.

Liquorice Allsorts were originally intended to be sold as individual flavours and met with little enthusiasm until Bassett's salesman Charlie Thompson accidentally dropped his samples one day. Seeing the sweets all mixed up, a Leicester wholesaler thought they looked far more appetising. Thompson had stumbled across a winner.

Unbelievable Facts

On average, Americans eat 18 acres of pizza a day.

Nutmeg is extremely poisonous if injected intravenously.

In the course of a year, 44 per cent of Americans go on a diet.

Tinned food was first introduced in 1812, but nobody got round to inventing a tin opener for another 50 years.

The world's oldest piece of chewing gum dates back over 9000 years.

To encourage contraception, some Danish restaurants began serving after-dinner condoms instead of mints.

104 million chickens are slaughtered every day worldwide.

In 4th-century Sparta, men over 20 were required by law to eat at least 2 lb of meat a day. This was supposed to make them brave.

In the Middle Ages, chicken soup was thought to be an aphrodisiac.

China's Beijing Duck Restaurant can seat 9000 people at one time.

The Greeks eat more bread per person than anyone else in the world.

Although salt is generally thought of as a seasoning, only five out of every 100 lb produced each year go to the dinner table.

Food and Drink

The national dish of the Faeroe Islands is puffin stuffed with rhubarb.

Herring is the most widely eaten fish in the world.

European herbalists of the Middle Ages feared that basil leaves harboured scorpions.

Blancmange was originally a savoury dish.

Cooks in the Italian town of Viareggio contend that a good soup must always contain a stone from the sea.

The largest item on any menu in the world is probably roast camel, a dish sometimes served at Bedouin wedding feasts. The camel is served with a sheep's carcass, which is stuffed with chickens, which are stuffed with fish, which are stuffed with eggs.

Alligator, bear's paws, curried fruit bat, rattlesnake and termites are all considered to be aphrodisiacs.

The first electric toasters could only toast one side of the bread at a time.

With beef unavailable because of the Franco-Prussian War, Parisians of the 1870s turned to horse meat instead.

McDonald's started out cooking hot dogs rather than hamburgers.

China has centres for recycling toothpicks.

Unbelievable Facts

If you were to rub garlic on the heel of your foot, it would be absorbed by the pores and eventually show up on your breath.

Eskimos use refrigerators to prevent food from freezing.

Tablecloths were originally intended to serve as towels on which guests could wipe their hands and face after dinner.

Honey is the only food that doesn't spoil. Alexander the Great's body was preserved in a jar of honey.

The Earl of Sandwich didn't invent the sandwich. One was eaten by Roman soldiers nearly 2000 years earlier.

The very first choc ice was called an Eskimo Pie.

Salmon was so cheap and plentiful in 18th-century America that some servants stipulated in their terms of employment that they would not be served salmon for dinner more than once a week.

As early as 4000 BC, the Egyptians were producing more than 40 types of bread.

Angered by a below-par meal, the 15th-century German emperor Wenceslas ordered his chef to be roasted alive on a spit.

First Lady Eleanor Roosevelt ate three chocolate-covered garlic balls every morning. Her doctor prescribed this diet to improve her memory.

Vinegar was the strongest acid known to the ancients.

Food and Drink

Subjects could buy tickets to watch George II and the royal family eat Sunday dinner.

In Georgian England, a meal of animals' testicles was considered to be an aphrodisiac.

In Japan, the meat from the spiny puffer fish is considered a rare delicacy. However the liver and intestines contain a powerful neurotoxin which can kill, so it is essential that the chef prepares the fish properly before serving.

The Romans ate plenty of parsley because they thought it prevented them from getting drunk.

The Romans thought it a sin to eat the flesh of a woodpecker.

In ancient China, mouse meat was a noted delicacy.

Peanuts are one of the ingredients in dynamite.

In Paris you used to be able to hire dinner party guests. These people were known as "quatorzes" because they were used to raise the numbers from an uneven 13 to a nicely balanced 14.

Flamingo tongues were a popular delicacy at Roman feasts.

A six-year-old Dorset boy became so addicted to Spam that he ate his way through six tins every week for three years. He was sent to a child psychiatrist.

Arachibutyrophobia is a fear of peanut butter sticking to the roof of your mouth.

Chop suey was invented in New York, not China.

In 1626, English philosopher Francis Bacon conducted one of the earliest experiments into frozen food. He stuffed a chicken with snow so that he could observe whether the cold helped to preserve the bird's flesh. Alas, he caught a fatal chill from handling so much snow.

Aristotle's favourite meat was camel meat.

When Mars Bars were first exported to the Soviet Union in 1991, the queues were so long that no customer was allowed to buy more than four.

200 years ago, chocolate was considered to be a temptation to the devil. In Central American mountain villages, no one under 60 was allowed to drink it and churchgoers who defied the ruling were threatened with excommunication.

Every time you lick a stamp, you consume one-tenth of a calorie.

Somewhere in the world, a tin of Spam is opened every four seconds.

The ice lolly was invented by an 11-year-old boy. Young Frank Epperson left a container of soda and a stirrer outside one night and in the morning discovered that they had frozen together. The first drink on a stick was called the Epsicle in his honour.

In 1992, a Dutch café owner made an ice lolly weighing 12,346 lb. What did he use as a stick?

Popcorn was banned in most American cinemas in 1920 because it was too noisy.

The first supermarket chain in the United States was called Piggly Wiggly. It was in 1916 that one Clarence Saunders introduced check-outs and a turnstile entrance at his Piggly Wiggly store in Memphis. It proved such a success that within seven years, a further 2800 Piggly Wigglies sprang up across the US.

In Britain alone, over 8000 people a year are treated in hospital for injuries caused by supermarket trolleys.

Popcorn kernels were found in the graves of ancient Indians.

50 gallons of maple sap are needed to make a single gallon of maple syrup.

Sausages were banned in Rome by the Christian emperor Constantine the Great because of their link to pagan festivities.

Unbelievable Facts

Louis XVI was such a chocoholic that he employed a special courtier whose principal duty was to keep the king supplied with chocolate.

The world's hen population lays over two billion eggs per day, which would make an omelette the size of Cyprus.

Whereas the spoon dates back thousands of years, the fork was not invented until the 11th century, and was not accepted until the 18th century. For centuries, clergymen had condemned the use of the fork, arguing that only human fingers, created by God, should touch God's bounty. Also, the use of a fork by men was considered effeminate. Finally in the 18th century, aristocrats used forks at separate place settings to distinguish themselves from the lower classes who still shared bowls and glasses.

Rubber is one of the ingredients of bubble gum.

Even in the 18th century, many dinner guests brought their own cutlery because none was provided by their hosts.

Only about a third of the world's population eats with a knife and fork.

Foods like yoghurt which coalesce are invaluable for astronauts. In the weightlessness of space, while the spoon may float off, the yoghurt will stay on it.

Anne Boleyn used to throw up between courses. She employed a lady-in-waiting whose job it was to hold up a sheet whenever the queen began to turn green.

James I's tongue was too large for his mouth. So he used to slobber his food all over the table.

Cheese Dips

Blue Vinny cheese is so hard that a whole cheese was once used as a temporary replacement for a wheel on a train.

The main reason the Romans built a wall around Chester was to protect the city's cheese industry.

Three hundred tons of Cheshire cheese were sent to Royalist troops in Scotland during the Civil War.

There are no fewer than 216 varieties of cheese in France.

The French King Charlemagne insisted on having two mule loads of Roquefort sent to his palace every Christmas.

A 1956 expedition to the South Pole found a tin of Edam left behind by Captain Scott and his party in 1912. The cheese was still fit to eat.

In the 12th century, Blanche of Navarre tried to win the heart of French King Philippe Auguste by sending him 200 cheeses each year.

Cheese was a form of currency in 16th-century Denmark and was used to pay church taxes.

Blue Cheshire was once used for treating sores and wounds.

Cornish Yarg cheese is served coated in nettles.

The French cheese Gaperon used to be hung from kitchen windows to ripen.

Bottoms Up!

It has been estimated that, at any given time, 0.7 per cent of the world's population are drunk.

Dom Perignon, after whom the champagne is named, was a blind Benedictine monk.

A raisin dropped in a glass of champagne will bounce up and down continually inside the glass.

On a royal hunting trip to Egypt, Edward VII's entourage took 7,000 bottles of wine.

In medieval England, beer was often served with breakfast.

Every day, British Prime Minister William Pitt the Younger used to drink six bottles of port, two bottles of Madeira and a bottle and a half of claret. He was often hopelessly drunk in the House of Commons and would disappear behind the Speaker's chair in mid-debate to throw up.

When the Luxembourg branch of Alcoholics Anonymous was founded in 1948, there were just two members.

A 1974 dinner dance for the Belfast branch of Alcoholics Anonymous ended in a brawl after £375 had been spent at the bar.

France produces 22 million bottles of wine a day.

Vodka sales comprise ten per cent of the Russian government's income.

Coca-Cola was originally green.

At an extravagant party during the reign of William III, the Hon Edward Russell used the fountain in his garden as a giant punch bowl for mixing drinks. The ingredients included 560 gallons of brandy, 1300 lb of sugar, 25,000 lemons, 20 gallons of lime juice and 5 lb of nutmeg. Russell's butler rowed around the fountain in a small boat, filling the punch cups for the guests.

Iceland consumes more Coca-Cola per head than any other nation.

The first person to taste coffee was an Ethiopian shepherd who noticed that his sheep stayed awake all night after grazing on coffee berries. The shepherd ate some berries and found that they had the same effect on him.

Adverts for coffee in 1657 claimed that it was an effective cure for scurvy, gout and a variety of other ailments.

King Gustav III, 18th-century ruler of Sweden, was so convinced that coffee was poisonous that he ordered a criminal to drink himself to death with coffee. The execution was less than successful, the condemned man eventually dying of old age.

In 16th- and 17th-century Turkey, anyone caught drinking coffee was put to death.

Frederick the Great used to drink coffee made with champagne instead of water.

When Nescafé was launched in Britain in 1939, one of Nestlés leading salesmen remarked: "It will never sell – the British only drink tea."

It takes approximately 2000 berries to make 1 lb of coffee.

The world's most expensive coffee is made from a bean which has been passed by a cat. The droppings of the palm civet, which lives in the coffee plantations of Sumatra, are highly prized for their flavour. In Japan, the resultant coffee sells for around £10 a cup.

Milk from young coconuts was used as blood plasma during the Second World War.

Yak's milk is pink.

Coca-Cola was originally devised as a brain tonic.

When advertising men for Pepsi-Cola had their slogan "Come alive with Pepsi" translated into Mandarin Chinese, it came over as "Pepsi brings your ancestors back from the grave".

The average person will consume 12,000 gallons of water in a lifetime.

Novelist Arnold Bennett drank a glass of water in a Paris hotel in 1931 to prove that it was safe. He died two months later from typhoid.

Food and Drink

Right up until the 19th century, urine was often used as an early-morning mouthwash.

The average Chinese person has just eight soft drinks a year.

Tea was once used as currency in Siberia.

Enough tea leaves are produced every day to make three billion cups of tea.

Victorian Prime Minister William Gladstone used to fill his stone hot-water bottle with tea. Since he rarely slept for more than four hours, when he woke up, the tea was still warm enough to drink.

When tea was first introduced to the US, women, in their ignorance, served the tea leaves with sugar or syrup after throwing away the water in which the leaves had been boiled.

On average, every glass of London tap water has previously passed through nine other people.

Perrier water bottles were modelled on the shape of Indian clubs. Recuperating from a car accident, Englishman St John Harmsworth, brother of newspaper magnates Lord Northcliffe and Lord Rothermere, visited the French spa town of Vergeze in 1903. There he was introduced by his doctor, Louis Perrier, to the local spring, said to have been discovered by Hannibal. Recognizing the commercial possibilities of the water, Harmsworth decided to purchase the spring and bottle it. He named the water after Dr Perrier and moulded the now famous green Perrier bottle on the Indian clubs he had been using to strengthen his arms and back following the accident.

More people are allergic to cow's milk than any other food.

Ovaltine got its name thanks to a clerical error. It was launched as Ovomaltine in 1904 (it contains eggs and malt), but when the Wander company applied to register the trade mark five years later, it was wrongly transcribed by a ministry clerk as "Ovaltine". The name stuck.

MAD SCIENTISTS, WACKY INVENTIONS AND WILD WEATHER

Inventive Minds

In 1875, the director of the US Patent Office tendered his resignation and suggested that the department be closed on the grounds that there was nothing left to invent.

The world's first photograph was taken in 1826. Ironically the man behind it, Frenchman Nicéphore Niepce, was almost blind.

Laszlo Biro, the brains behind the ball-point pen, lost a fortune by forgetting to patent his invention in the US.

The first ball-point pens to go on sale in Britain in 1946 cost £2 15s each.

The first pair of roller skates were the brainchild of Belgian musician Joseph Merlin. Keen to impress guests at a ball in London in 1760, Merlin made a grand entry on his skates while playing the violin. But, unable to stop or change direction, he shot across the ballroom straight into a full-length mirror and was badly injured.

When Joseph Gayetty invented toilet paper in 1857, he had his name printed on each sheet.

Wallace Carothers, the man who invented nylon, committed suicide before the first products hit the market.

The stethoscope was born out of shyness. Young French physician René Laennec had to examine a pretty woman with a heart condition. The usual practice in the early 19th century was for a doctor to listen to the patient's heartbeat by placing his ear next to her bare chest. But Laennec felt too embarrassed and so he used a rolled-up newspaper instead. Intrigued to find that the tubular shape magnified the sounds, he went on to construct a wooden cylinder — the world's first stethoscope.

The cigarette lighter was invented before the safety match.

Bullet proof vests, fire escapes and windscreen wipers were all invented by women.

When sticky envelopes were first introduced in the 19th century, they were unpopular because many people thought it was an insult to send their saliva to someone else.

Hovercraft inventor Christopher Cockerell built his prototype model from an empty tin of cat food, a coffee tin and a vacuum cleaner.

The ancient Etruscans of Italy were the first people to eat with false teeth — some 2700 years ago. They used rows of animal teeth, held together with strips of gold.

The world's first cash dispenser was opened at Barclays Bank, Enfield, in 1967 by *On the Buses* star Reg Varney.

A device invented as a primitive steam engine by Greek engineer Hero at around the time of the birth of Jesus is used as the basis for modern rotating lawn sprinklers.

The first electric kettles took 12 minutes to boil.

The idea for Velcro came to Georges de Mestral while he was out hunting. He noticed that that his trousers and the ears of his dog were covered in burrs, picked up by brushing against burdock weed. On returning home, de Mestral examined the tenacious little burrs under the microscope and observed their numerous tiny hooks. Recalling how a jammed zip on his wife's dress had ruined an evening out, he set about re-creating the hooked surface of the burr in textile form and came up with a new kind of fastener.

Enough Velcro is produced each year to stretch twice around the world.

James Watt, pioneer of the steam engine, was twice arrested for flashing.

One of the earliest attempts at suntan cream was prepared by American pharmacist Benjamin Green who cooked cocoa butter in a coffee pot on his wife's stove and applied the solution to his head.

Percy Shaw became a millionaire through his invention of the cat's eye but he lived in a house which had neither carpets nor curtains. He thought that carpets harboured unpleasant smells and that curtains would restrict his view of his beloved Yorkshire.

The fax machine was invented before the telephone. The first fax machines were around in the 1840s – 30 years before Bell's invention.

The first hearing aid weighed 16 lb and had to be placed on the user's lap or on an adjacent table.

Swede Alfred Nobel, who gives his name to the Nobel Peace Prize, was the inventor of dynamite.

A French inventor who tried to perfect the world's first vacuum cleaner merely succeeded in blowing himself up. His widow was also obliged to pay for repairs to property over a large area of Lyon.

The first video recorder in 1956 was the size of a piano.

The dishwasher was invented as early as 1855.

The first commercial vacuum cleaner was the brainchild of Hubert Cecil Booth. It was extremely noisy and frightened passing horses, which led to Booth being sued by cab proprietors. It was also so big that it had to be mounted on a wagon. The making of Booth's invention was the 1902 coronation of Edward VII at which the vacuum cleaned the blue carpets of Westminster Abbey. The king and queen were sufficiently impressed to order two cleaners – one for Buckingham Palace, the other for Windsor Castle. The vacuum cleaner quickly became a novelty. Society hostesses threw parties in their homes so that guests could watch it in action.

The safety razor first went on sale in the US in 1903. But it was hardly an instant success, only 51 razors being sold in the entire country in the first 12 months.

Paul Winchell, the voice of Tigger in *Winnie the Pooh* films, invented the artificial heart.

The pioneering answerphone in Britain was the Ipsophone, manufactured in Switzerland. It weighed a mighty 2½ cwt and took two men as long as three days to install.

Paper was invented by a Chinese eunuch.

The first flush toilet system was invented in 1596 for Queen Elizabeth I. But it was not until the 1880s that it was perfected by a Doncaster plumber by the name of . . . Thomas Crapper.

The electric chair was invented by a dentist.

Slot machines date back to 100 BC. They were used for dispensing holy water.

German chemist Christian Schönbein founded the modern explosives industry in his wife's kitchen. It was while working there in 1845 that he accidentally spilt a mixture of nitric and sulphuric acid on to a cotton apron. He hung the apron up to dry, but as soon as it dried out, it exploded. To make up for the loss of his apron, Schönbein had stumbled across nitro-cellulose. By 1890, nitro-cellulose, in the form of gun cotton, had replaced gunpowder as the most effective military explosive.

The comb dates back to Scandinavia around 8000 BC.

Light bulb inventor Thomas Edison was afraid of the dark. Although by the time he died, he held nearly 1300 patents, Edison only had three months of schooling in his entire life.

American Chester Greenwood was just 15 when he invented earmuffs.

Scottish physicist James Clerk Maxwell used to test his theories by engaging in deep scientific discussions with his dog Tobi.

Patently Absurd

Essex inventor Terry Convoy has designed a device which automatically replaces a toilet seat after it has been used. He has spent five years and over £15,000 perfecting the battery-powered seat and hopes that it will put the lid on women's complaints.

In 1902, Andrew Jackson Jr of Tennessee patented an eye protector for chickens to stop them being hen-pecked. The protector was in the form of a pair of miniature glasses.

In the 1980s, three Frenchwomen marketed a musical nappy. Thanks to a device tucked inside, as soon as the nappy became wet, it played "When the Saints Go Marching In".

Back in 1914 Natalie Stolp of Philadelphia devised an implement designed to discourage men from rubbing their thighs up against those of a lady on a crowded train or carriage. She patented a spring attached to the lady's underskirt which responded to male pressure by releasing a short, sharp point into the offender's flesh.

In 1907, Ignatius Nathaniel Soares of Massachusetts came up with a device designed to improve the shape of your nose.

To reduce pedestrian casualties in 1960, American David Gutman invented a special bumper designed to be fixed to the front of a car. Not only did it cushion the impact but it also had a huge pair of claws which grabbed the pedestrian around the waist to prevent him from falling to the ground.

In 1967, Harold W. Dahly of Chicago patented a solar-cooled hat which operated by means of a solar-powered fan discreetly positioned inside the headgear.

Finland's George Carlson devised a poultry disinfector in 1919. It cleaned the birds' bottoms by dusting them with insecticide powder.

In 1994 Italian Lini Missio patented a condom that played Beethoven whenever it tore during use.

Earl M. Christopherson of Seattle patented a 1960 device to enable people to look inside their own ears.

The Loving Cup bra of 1979 contained a tiny electronic circuit which signalled when it was safe for sex. Its lights flashed red or green indicating whether sex could result in pregnancy.

US Patent No. 4734078 is for a bra which surrounds the breasts with water so that a buoyant force provides improved and independent support for each breast. A transparent version is suggested for those who wish to make a fashion statement.

An American inventor has come up with a kissing shield. A thin, latex membrane which covers the mouth in a heart-shaped frame, the shield serves as a germ barrier and is particularly recommended for politicians who have to kiss a lot of babies.

In 1966 American Thomas J. Bayard invented a vibrating toilet seat, acting on the belief that physical stimulation of the buttocks is effective in relieving constipation.

Baffled with Science

Granite conducts sound ten times faster than air.

In its liquid form, mercury can be poured out of a jug and yet leave the inside of the jug completely dry.

There are as many molecules in a spoonful of water as there are spoonfuls of water in the Atlantic Ocean.

No piece of square dry paper can be folded in half more than seven times.

When glass breaks, the fragments can move as fast as 3000 mph.

Nickel was named after a German goblin.

If you swing a bucket of water round and round above your head, the water will stay in it even when the bucket is upside down. The water's inertia tells it to continue rushing through space at a steady speed in a straight line and, having been started in one direction by the swinging bucket, to carry on in that direction. Since the bucket is made to follow a circular path, the water is forced to accelerate to get round the corners. This gives it "artificial gravity" which makes it stick to the bottom of the bucket even when the bucket is upside down.

A cubic foot of the metal osmium weighs 1410 lb – the equivalent of ten people each weighing ten stone.

Isaac Newton named seven colours in the spectrum even though indigo is barely distinguishable as a separate colour, because seven was his favourite number.

The ancient Greeks conducted experiments to try and turn lead into gold.

Hot water weighs more than cold.

Water has a greater molecular density in liquid form than as a solid. That's why ice floats.

The first antibiotics were developed in ancient Egypt where patients were treated with mouldy bread.

It is estimated that a plastic container can resist decomposition for 50,000 years.

All the gold ever mined in the world would only make a block roughly the size of a tennis court.

Crystals grow by reproduction, making them the closest to being "alive" of all minerals.

A lump of pure gold the size of a matchbox can be flattened into a sheet the size of a tennis court.

As a child, French mathematician Blaise Pascal locked himself in his room for several days and wouldn't allow anyone to enter. When he finally emerged, he had worked out all of Euclid's geometrical theorems for himself.

Descartes came up with the theory of co-ordinate geometry from watching a fly walk across a tiled ceiling.

Arabic numerals were invented in India.

One sum is always the same, whatever the numbers. Take any three-figure number in which the first figure is larger than the last – for example 834. Then reverse it, making 438, and subtract the smaller number from the larger, making 396. Finally add that to the same number reversed, in this case 693. The answer is 1089, and will be 1089 whatever the starting number.

When written in Roman numerals, the year 1666 (MDCLXVI) is the only date in history that is written from highest to lowest value. M = 1000, D = 500, C = 100, L = 50, X = 10, V = 5, I = 1.

The Body Beautiful
Every night while you're asleep, you grow by about 0.3 inches, but shrink again in the morning. This is because pressure on the cartilage discs in the spine is relieved during sleep, allowing the discs to expand.

It is impossible to sneeze with your eyes open. A sneeze travels at over 100 mph.

When you sneeze, all your bodily functions stop momentarily — even your heart.

The total body heat produced by a human in a day is sufficient to power a light bulb for a day and a half.

There is enough hydrochloric acid in your digestive system to dissolve a steel nail.

The human stomach lining replaces itself every three days.

Before all-porcelain false teeth were perfected in the 19th century, dentures were usually made with teeth pulled from the mouths of soldiers who had been killed in battle.

If you lock your knee for long enough while standing, you'll eventually pass out.

When you walk, the amount of pressure you exert on each thighbone is equivalent to the weight of an adult elephant.

Every day, the average person releases nearly a pint of intestinal gas by flatulence.

If you pass wind continually for six years and nine months, you'll produce enough gas to create an atomic bomb.

The human brain continues to send out electrical wave signals for up to 37 hours after death.

There is enough fat in the human body to make seven bars of soap.

Unbelievable Facts

It would cost over £5 billion to programme and sell a computer which could do all the things a human brain does.

We only use 10 per cent of our brains.

Artificial limbs date back to around 1500 BC.

Human thigh bones are stronger than concrete.

You're born with 300 bones, but as an adult you only have 206.

The human body contains sufficient sulphur to kill the fleas on a dog.

Those two lines that connect your top lip to the bottom of your nose are known as the philtrum.

A quarter of the bones in your body are in your feet.

If you're locked in a completely sealed room, you'll die of carbon dioxide poisoning before you'll die of oxygen starvation.

During menstruation, the sensitivity of a woman's middle finger is reduced.

It takes 17 facial muscles to smile but 43 to frown.

One brow wrinkle is the result of approximately 200,000 frowns.

Raising your eyebrows uses over 30 muscles.

Our noses and ears never stop growing.

Ingrown toenails are hereditary.

There are 4000 wax glands in the human ear.

Apparently it only takes 7 lb of pressure to tear off your ear. But don't try this at home . . .

If all the iron in the human body were collected together, there would be enough to make a medium-sized nail.

The average person falls asleep at night in seven minutes.

Human muscular strength reaches a peak at the age of 25. After that, it starts to go into decline.

The muscles on the sides of your mouth allow you to bite into things with a force of 160 lb — equivalent to the weight of 18 house bricks.

Most people produce enough spit in a lifetime to fill two swimming pools.

You can't kill yourself by holding your breath.

The short-term memory capacity for most people is between five and nine numbers.

It's official: women get drunk quicker than men. This is because women's bodies are 58 per cent water whereas men's are 70 per cent, the extra water helping to dilute the alcohol.

There are more signal connections in the human brain than there would be in a telephone exchange connecting everyone in the world.

Unbelievable Facts

The tooth is the only part of the human body which can't repair itself.

During pregnancy, a woman's uterus expands to over 30 times its normal weight.

The human body contains enough phosphorus to make 2200 match heads.

The average brain comprises a mere two per cent of a person's total body weight, yet it requires 25 per cent of all the oxygen used by the body.

The most sensitive cluster of nerves in the human body is at the base of the spine.

The human nose is only one-twentieth as sensitive as that of a dog.

By the age of 70, half of your taste buds will have gone.

There are more bacteria in your mouth than there are people in the world.

Over 100 different viruses cause the common cold.

The average person will pass about 8800 gallons of urine in a lifetime. This is enough to fill 500 baths – but who'd want to sit in them?

The Neanderthal's brain was bigger than yours is.

If your lungs were laid out flat, they would cover an area the size of a tennis court.

An adult's liver weighs about the same as half a dozen medium-sized oranges.

The average human body contains enough potassium to fire a toy cannon.

People with mental disorders rarely yawn.

On average, you flex your finger joints 25 million times in your lifetime.

The human left lung is smaller than the right to make room for the heart. Consequently the right lung takes in more air than the left.

Fingernails grow four times faster than toenails. Both grow faster in warm weather than cold.

Your brain is more active while you're sleeping than it is while you're watching TV.

Your body contains enough water to fill at least three large buckets.

The average human body contains enough carbon to make 900 pencils.

Particularly sensitive people can detect sweetness in a solution which is one part sugar to 200 parts water. Yet certain moths and butterflies can detect sweetness when the ratio is one to 300,000.

Right-handed people live nine years longer, on average, than left-handers.

A woman's heart beats faster than a man's.

If you are right-handed, the nails on your right hand will grow faster than those on your left, and vice versa.

In an average lifetime, a person will walk the equivalent of five times around the equator.

Sound and Vision

A typical issue of a broadsheet newspaper contains around 100,000 words. To read it all, your eyes must travel over half a mile.

The human ear can pick out more than 1500 musical tones.

Men are more likely than women to suffer from colour-blindness. Whereas seven men in 100 are at least partly colour-blind, only one woman in 1000 is.

Blue eyes get paler with age.

It takes human eyes an hour to adapt to seeing properly in the dark. Once adapted, they are about 100,000 times more sensitive to light than they are in bright sunlight.

Relative to size, the strongest muscle in the human body is the tongue. Everyone has a different tongue print.

It requires the interaction of 72 different muscles to produce human speech.

If you go blind in one eye, you'll only lose about one fifth of your vision.

Your eye muscles move more than 100,000 times a day.

The hyoid, a v-shaped bone located at the base of the tongue between the mandible and the voice box, is the only bone in the human body not connected to another. Its job is to support the tongue and its muscles.

Women blink nearly twice as much as men. On average, we spend 23 minutes a day blinking.

The average talker sprays about 300 microscopic saliva droplets per minute — that's something like two and a half droplets per word.

The sound of a snore can be almost as loud as a pneumatic drill.

The pop which you hear when you crack your knuckles is actually a bubble of gas bursting.

Laughing is good exercise. It provides a workout for the diaphragm and increases the body's ability to use oxygen.

Skin Deep

You shed and re-grow your outer skin cells approximately every 27 days, which means you will have nearly 1000 new skins in a lifetime.

In an average lifetime, a person will shed 40 lb of skin.

If it was collected in a pile, the total skin covering of an adult would weigh about 6 lb.

The most sensitive skin is on your fingertips, toes and lips. There are 20 times more cold detectors in your lips than in your legs.

Most dust particles in the house consist of dead skin.

On average, a pair of human feet lose half a pint of water in perspiration each day.

Perspiration is odourless. It's the bacteria on the skin which create the smell.

Blood Brothers

The total length of blood vessels in the human body is an incredible 62,000 miles — enough to stretch nearly two and a half times around the equator.

The rarest blood group in the world is a type of Bombay blood known as H-H. Only three people have ever been found with it.

To combat disease, your body produces 10 billion new white blood cells every day.

15 million blood cells are destroyed in the human body every second.

The sound you hear when you hold a seashell to your ear is that of your blood pumping.

The human heart creates enough pressure when it pumps out to the body to squirt blood a distance of 30 ft.

In your lifetime you pump out enough blood to fill the fuel tanks of 800 jumbo jets.

It only takes a minute for a blood cell to travel all around your body and back to your heart.

Your heart beats about 100,000 times a day.

There are 30 billion red blood cells in your body. New red cells are made at a rate of about three million a second.

Red blood cells live for around four months. So in its short life-time, a red blood cell will have circulated around your body over 170,000 times.

Split Ends

It has been estimated that an adult man of average weight could be lifted up by a rope made from just 100 human hairs.

Blondes not only have more fun, they have more hairs on their head. Blondes have 140,000 hairs on average, compared to 110,000 if you've got brown or black hair, and 90,000 if you're a redhead.

A single hair can hold the weight of a large apple.

Beards are the fastest growing hairs on the human body. If a man never trimmed his beard, it would grow to a length of almost 30 ft in an average lifetime.

On average, we lose between 30 and 60 hairs every day.

Hair grows slowest at night. And it grows faster in the summer than in winter.

If all the eyelashes you shed in your life were joined together, they would form a strand over 100 ft long.

At any given time, 90 per cent of scalp hairs are growing – the remainder are resting.

You need to lose over half of your scalp hairs before anyone starts to notice that you're going thin on top.

Human eyelashes live for about 150 days.

In the course of an average lifetime, you will grow 6½ ft of nose hair. So it's best to keep those trimmers handy.

There are 30,000 whiskers on the face of the average man.

In the course of his life, a clean-shaven man will spend 3350 hours with a razor in his hand.

Size Isn't Everything

The average duration of sexual intercourse for humans is a mere two minutes.

100 million acts of sexual intercourse take place throughout the world every day.

On average, most men experience erections every 75 minutes while they're asleep.

The maximum speed at which erotic sensations travel from the skin to the brain has been measured at 156 mph.

A man will ejaculate, on average, 7200 times in his life – 2000 of these will be from masturbation.

In the course of an average lifetime, a man will produce 14 gallons of semen – enough to fill nine good-sized watering cans.

The speed of an ejaculation has been measured at 28 mph. That's 3 mph faster than a city bus, although there's not room for quite as many people on top.

Sex burns 360 calories per hour. Per hour???!!!

The men of Ancient Egypt rubbed crocodile dung into their penises in the hope of making them bigger.

Leading up to the Second World War, most condoms were imported from Germany. So when war broke out, British soldiers were preparing for action stations wearing German condoms.

Birth-control campaigns in Egypt in the late 1970s foundered because village women preferred to wear the Pill in a locket as a talisman.

The first contraceptive diaphragm consisted of half an orange rind.

The Japanese used to wear condoms made from tortoiseshell . . . presumably to increase their staying power.

Such was the demand for contraception in Macclesfield that the drains were blocked by thousands of used condoms.

You burn 26 calories in a one-minute kiss.

It would take the average couple over four years to try every one of the 529 positions in the *Kama Sutra*.

Baby Talk

The average new-born baby spends 133 minutes a day crying.

Babies are born without knee-caps. They don't appear until between the ages of two and six.

A new-born baby's head accounts for about a quarter of its body weight.

A foetus acquires fingerprints at the age of three months.

Children born in May are, on average, 200 grams heavier at birth than those born in any other month.

Even if both parents are midgets or dwarfs, they will invariably produce normal-sized children.

Human babies start dreaming before they're born.

Up to the age of around six months, babies can breathe and swallow at the same time. This is something which adults can't do.

Twins are born less frequently in the eastern world than in the west.

First-born children tend to be higher achievers and more intelligent than later-born siblings.

Record Breakers

Robert Wadlow of Illinois was 8 ft 11 in tall when he died in 1940.

A woman in China was just over 8 ft tall when she died in 1982.

American Jon Brower Minnoch weighed 69 st 9 lb in 1976. When he was taken ill two years later, it took a dozen firemen to move him. In hospital he needed two beds strapped together and it required the efforts of 13 staff just to turn him over.

John Roy of Clacton began growing a moustache in 1939 and by 1976, it was 74½ in wide. He accidentally sat on it in the bath a few years later and lost 16½ in.

After not cutting the fingernails on his left hand for 44 years, the average length of Indian Shridhar Chillal's nails was 46 inches. His thumbnail was 52 inches long.

When he died in 1927, Norwegian Hans Langseth had a beard 17 ft 6 in long.

Curious Cures

A popular cure for whooping cough in 19th-century Yorkshire was to drink a soup containing nine frogs. But apparently it only worked if the patient didn't know in advance what was lurking in the soup. An alternative remedy was to feed the sufferer with milk which had previously been partly lapped by a ferret.

Passing a child three times under the belly of a donkey was also believed to cure whooping cough.

Binding the temples with a rope with which a man has been hanged was once thought to be a good cure for a headache.

Wearing an elder twig in your ear night and day was once supposed to cure deafness.

In medieval times, the cure for meningitis was to split a pigeon in half and lay the two parts, cut side down, on top of the patient's head.

In ancient Carthage, it was believed that rubbing a cow's tail on your stomach would cure indigestion.

The cure for convulsions in medieval Britain was to take a slice of fingernail, a few hairs plucked from the eyebrows and the crown of the head, and to tie them together in a cloth. The bundle, with a halfpenny added for good measure, was then left at a crossroads, and whoever picked it up was believed to take on the disease. For obvious reasons, people were reluctant to pick up strange-looking parcels at crossroads.

The Romans used to cure toothache by strapping toads to their jaws.

In the 18th century, Prussian surgeons treated stutterers by cutting off portions of their tongues.

Shock treatment for epilepsy was once administered by means of an electric catfish.

An early form of tomato ketchup was a popular tonic for the cure of diarrhoea in the late 19th century.

Carrying a child through a flock of sheep was said to cure respiratory problems.

Back in the 15th century, anyone ill was invariably dressed in red because it was thought this would help them towards a speedy recovery.

A popular 17th-century cure for toothache was to apply sweat from the anus of a cat which had just been chased across a ploughed field.

The court physician of Louis XVIII was terrified of draughts. He wouldn't allow anyone to open windows while he was in the room. He travelled everywhere wrapped up in blankets and with a clove of garlic in each ear and nostril. The measures seemed to work for he outlived most of his contemporaries.

Writer Alexandre Dumas suffered from terrible insomnia. He tried all sorts of remedies, including eating an apple under the Arc de Triomphe.

A popular medieval cure for rheumatism was to carry a dead shrew in your pocket.

Tudor men believed that rubbing horse urine into the scalp prevented baldness.

If a Roman barber accidentally cut his customer, he would treat the nick with a spider's web soaked in vinegar.

Bathing in the wash water of a corpse was rumoured to cure epileptic fits.

The Irish cure for mumps was to lead the patient three times around a pigsty.

Throwing a dung beetle over your shoulder used to be a familiar cure for stomach ache.

In the 16th century being breathed on by a billy goat was thought to grant protection from the plague.

An apparently effective, though unsociable, cure for tuberculosis in olden days was to shove your head into the carcass of a freshly-slaughtered cow (preferably while the cow's body was still steaming), pull the folds of flesh up around your neck and inhale.

During the Second World War, Marmite was prescribed as a cure for tropical diseases such as burning feet and beriberi. And a 1951 report on Deficiency Diseases in Japanese Prison Camps stated that Marmite had proved effective in the treatment of scrotal dermatitis. The patients were presumably the original "Marmite soldiers".

Out Of This World
An astronaut orbiting Earth sees the sun rise and set 15 times a day.

Jupiter's years are 12 times longer than those of Earth.

A day on Mercury is longer than its year. This is because Mercury takes longer to spin on its axis than it does to orbit the Sun. On the other hand, a Jupiter year is the length of some 10,400 Jupiter days.

Due to the time it takes light to reach Earth, the sun has been up for around eight minutes before we actually get to see it.

Unlike other planets in the solar system, Venus spins east to west instead of west to east.

The clouds on Venus are of sulphuric acid.

The last member of a group of people who were convinced that the Earth was hollow only died 18 years ago.

Although Mercury has daytime surface temperatures as high as 800°F, it has ice at its poles.

Driving at 70 mph, it would take 275 days to drive round one of Saturn's rings.

Bailly Crater on the Moon is 188 miles wide – almost as great as the distance between London and Paris.

Ganymede, the largest of Jupiter's moons, has a surface of ice some 60 miles thick.

Triton, a moon of Neptune, is the coldest known place in our solar system. Its surface temperature is −391°F.

A day on Venus is longer than a year on Earth.

Unbelievable Facts

The density of Saturn is so low that, if it fell into a huge area of water, it would float.

Jupiter is over twice as large as all of the other planets in the solar system put together.

In 1943, one sunspot lasted for 200 days – from June to December.

Earth spins so fast on its axis that someone standing on the equator is actually travelling at the speed of Concorde . . . without moving at all.

The next total eclipse in London will not occur until 5 May 2600. However on 14 June 2151, an eclipse will be 99 per cent total in London, and total on a line stretching from Belfast to Dover.

An object weighing 100 lb on Earth would only weigh 38 lb on Mars. On Mars you would be able to jump three times as high as you would on Earth.

Because of the difference in gravity, the men's world long jump record (just over 29 ft on Earth) would be 176 ft on the Moon, but only 11 ft on Jupiter.

Astronauts are unable to cry in space. Tears can't flow because of the lack of gravity.

An astronaut's heart gets smaller in space.

Since Uranus is tilted on its axis at around 98 degrees – almost on its side – it has the longest seasons in the solar system. Winters and summers on Uranus are the equivalent of 21 Earth years.

The Olympus Mons volcano on Mars is some 350 miles wide and 16 miles high.

At over 1200 mph, wind speeds on Neptune can be six times faster than the strongest hurricanes on Earth.

If you tried to count the stars in the galaxy at the rate of one per second, it would take 3000 years to count them all.

Night temperatures on Mars can plunge to as low as −48°F.

Neptune takes 165 Earth years to orbit the Sun. It was first seen in 1846 and so it won't return to the position in which it was first discovered until 2011.

The average temperature of the coldest place on Earth, Antarctica, is about four times warmer than the daytime temperature on Pluto.

Only 59 per cent of the Moon's surface is directly visible from Earth.

The Moon is about as wide as Australia.

There are roughly 18 stars in the Milky Way for each person on Earth.

All the coal, gas, oil and wood resources on Earth would only keep the Sun burning for a few days.

In just one second, the Sun produces 35 million times the amount of electricity used by the whole of the USA in an average year.

Raining Sprats and Frogs

Live frogs were found inside two huge hailstones which fell on the town of Dubuque, Iowa, in 1882. Twelve years later, a gopher turtle encased in ice fell on Bovina, Mississippi, during a violent hailstorm.

Years before Clarence Birdseye made his name, the German town of Essen received an unexpected delivery of frozen fish. At the height of a storm in 1896, freshwater carp fell from the sky, sealed inside blocks of ice.

There was a human hailstorm in Germany in 1930. Five glider pilots, caught in a thundercloud over the Rhön mountains, baled out but were carried up and down within the super-cooled cloud. Finally they plummeted to earth, frozen within ice prisons. Only one survived.

A carpenter working on the roof of his house near Düsseldorf in 1951 was killed after being impaled by a 6 ft long shaft of ice which had fallen from the sky.

In 1962, a cow in Iowa "flew" nearly half a mile after being sucked up by a tornado.

Something fishy? The people of Aberdare in Wales could hardly believe their eyes one morning in 1859 when the town was hit by a sudden shower of fish. Dozens of minnow and smooth-tailed stickleback landed in the streets.

During torrential rain, several hundred dead sand eels fell from the sky over the Hendon district of Sunderland in 1918.

Dozens of live frogs fell on Leicester, Massachusetts, in September 1953. Many were found in gutters and on roofs — proof that they had plunged from the sky.

A shower of large yellow mice fell on the Norwegian town of Bergen in 1578.

Pieces of meat fell from a cloudless sky over an area of Kentucky in 1876. When examined, the meat turned out to be lung and muscle tissue, either from a child or a horse. It was initially thought that the meat had been disgorged by flying buzzards, but this theory was later discounted.

Early one morning in 1896, a shower of dead birds — including ducks and woodpeckers — landed on the streets of Baton Rouge, Louisiana.

In 1911, a 2 ft long alligator fell from the sky at Evansville, Indiana, and landed on the front doorstep of a Mrs Hiram Winchell. When the stunned creature tried to crawl indoors, it was clubbed to death by Mrs Winchell and an army of neighbours.

Lumps of burning sulphur, some as big as a man's fist, dropped from the sky on to the roof of Loburg Castle in Germany during the summer of 1642.

Dollar bills fell from the sky over Chicago in 1975. A total of $588 was collected.

A fall of maggots accompanied a heavy storm at Acapulco, Mexico, in 1968. Craft gathered for the Olympic yachting events were covered in the insects.

A crop of hard, green peaches fell on a building site at Shreveport, Indiana, in 1961. And hundreds of golf balls descended from the sky and scored a direct hit on Punta Gorda, Florida, in 1969. Many roofs suffered minor damage and there was even a hole in one.

On 26 October 1956, the dead body of a small monkey was discovered in the back garden of a house at Broadmoor, California, by Mrs Faye Swanson. The post holding her clothes-line had been damaged, presumably by the falling monkey. It was suggested that the monkey may have fallen from a passing aircraft, but the local airport insisted that no planes had been carrying any monkeys at the time.

Blame It On The Weatherman

At any given time, 1800 thunderstorms are taking place somewhere in the world.

Tororo in Uganda experienced an average of 251 days of thunder per year over a 10-year period between 1967 and 1976.

In July 1949 a sudden blast of hot air swept across an area of Portugal, causing temperatures to shoot up from 100 to 150°F degrees Fahrenheit in only two minutes. The hot flush killed numerous chickens on local farms.

The British winter of 1435 was so cold that wagons were able to ride on the River Thames as far downstream as Gravesend.

Between October 1923 and April 1924 the temperature at Marble Bar in Western Australia reached a minimum of 100°F on 160 consecutive days. At Wyndham, also in Western Australia, the temperature reached 90°F or more on 333 days in 1946.

At Spearfish, South Dakota, in January 1943, the temperature rose from a freezing −4°F to a mild 45°F in just two minutes.

Ballynahinch in County Galway recorded 309 days of rain in 1923.

A total of 366 inches of rain fell in one month at Cherrapunji in India in 1861.

London had snow as early as 25 September in 1885 and as late as 2 June in 1975.

The winter of 1932 was so cold in America that the Niagara Falls froze solid.

Lightning strikes somewhere on Earth 100 times a second.

The longest lightning flashes have been measured at 20 miles. The smallest are thought to be less than 300 ft long.

A lightning bolt generates temperatures five times hotter than can be found on the surface of the Sun.

The eye of a tropical storm is completely calm.

There is sufficient energy in one bolt of lightning to power a home for two weeks.

The Empire State Building is hit by lightning some 500 times a year. It was once hit 12 times in 20 minutes.

On 13 September 1922 the shade temperature at al'Aziziyah in the Libyan desert reached 136°F – hot enough to fry an egg on a rock.

During exceptionally high winds, the Empire State Building has been known to sway several feet to either side.

Every second, a hurricane releases as much energy as the explosion of the atomic bomb which destroyed Hiroshima.

In ten minutes, a hurricane releases more energy than all of the world's nuclear weapons combined.

In Australia, a hurricane is called a "willy-willy".

It would take seven billion particles of fog to fill a teaspoon.

The winds inside cumulonimbus clouds may reach 124 mph.

A cumulonimbus cloud can be six miles across and 11 miles high – twice as high as Everest. A large specimen can hold enough water for 500,000 baths.

Most of the water droplets in a cloud re-evaporate and never reach the ground. Only one-fifth fall as rain.

A cold front travels at 30 mph – faster than Olympic sprinters can run.

No two snowflakes are identical.

The largest snowflake on record measured eight inches wide.

A politically incorrect California weather reporter was sacked recently for refusing to re-word "a chance of rain" to "a probability of sunshine" and "partly cloudy" to "largely sunny".

TRAINS AND BOATS AND PLANES

Trainspotting

When the first London Underground escalators were installed at Earls Court in 1911, a man with a wooden leg, "Bumper" Harris, was hired to ride up and down the escalators all day to reassure the public of their safety.

During 73 years of commuting to work by train from Birchington, near Margate, to London, Ralph Ransome travelled the equivalent of 39 times round the world.

Railway pioneer George Stephenson told MPs that trains would never go faster than 12 mph. This was to allay public fears that speeds of over 12 mph would bring about mental disorders among passengers.

The line between Lima and Huancayo in the Peruvian Andes reaches altitudes of over 15,000 ft. The air is so thin that railway officials bring round an oxygen trolley to tend to passengers who are feeling faint.

There are almost four miles of platforms at Waterloo station.

In the late 19th century, millions of human mummies were used as fuel for locomotives for Egypt. Wood and coal were in short supply at the time, but mummies were plentiful.

Less than half of the London Underground is actually underground.

The driver of a rush-hour InterCity train from Bristol to Swansea in 1997 managed to get hopelessly lost. He took the wrong route east of Neath and ended up taking the passengers on an unscheduled tour of the Welsh valleys. Half an hour later, he realized his error and pulled into a siding where the guard informed passengers that they were lost. An hour later, a new driver arrived to take the train back on the right line to Swansea.

In 1971 Mr and Mrs William Farmer of Margate travelled to Wales for their summer holiday. At the start of the week, they joined a British Rail mystery tour . . . which promptly took them straight back to Margate.

The longest stretch of straight railway track in the world is the one crossing Australia's Nullarbor Plain. It runs for 300 miles without so much as a curve.

The length of the US rail network would stretch nearly six times around the equator.

Daily commuter trains in Bombay are designed to carry 1700 passengers but regularly carry more than 7000.

In the 19th century, women travelling alone on trains used to place pins between their lips when entering tunnels in case strange men tried to kiss them in the dark.

Over 550 trains and 200,000 commuters pass through New York's Grand Central station every day.

The world's shortest rail network is in the Vatican City. It has just over half a mile of track.

The world's longest continuous railway line – the Trans-Siberian line from Moscow to Nakhodka – goes nearly a quarter of the way around the globe. There are 97 stops on the journey which is scheduled to take just over eight days.

In 1919 when there was a shortage of coal in Russian Turkestan, dried fish was used as locomotive fuel. On a branch of the Arica-La Paz Railway in Chile, engines were once powered by llama dung. And when there was a crop surplus in Brazil, coffee beans were used to power steam locomotives.

Up, Up and Away

The first passengers in the history of aviation were a cockerel, a sheep and a duck, transported by hot-air balloon in 1783. All emerged unscathed, except for the cockerel which was kicked by the sheep shortly before lift-off.

At any one time in the day, over a quarter of a million people are up in the air in planes.

The first cross-Channel balloon flight was made by two men stripped to their underpants. In 1785, Frenchman Jean-Pierre Blanchard persuaded wealthy American John Jeffries to join him in a flight from England to France. Six miles out from Dover, the balloon began to float perilously close to the sea so the duo jettisoned the flapping wings and rudder which were attached to the basket. Still struggling to gain height, they then decided to toss their coats into the sea. As the balloon continued to hover alarmingly close to the water, they realized that more drastic measures were needed to lighten the load. So they took off their trousers. That did the trick and they landed safely in France, wearing only their pants.

In 1865 an American designer suggested that a device powered by ten eagles could be used to transport a man through the air.

In 1910, escapologist Harry Houdini became the first person to fly a plane solo in Australia. Houdini taught himself to drive a car so that he could get to the airfield, but after that he never drove again.

The wingspan of a Boeing 747 is longer than the Wright Brothers' maiden flight.

To mark Air Force Week in 1975, a squadron of 30 Peruvian bombers swooped out of the sky for a demonstration attack on 14 abandoned fishing boats. After shelling the stationary targets for 15 minutes, the aircraft retired having failed to hit a single boat.

Trains and Boats and Planes

You could park 50 cars side by side on the wings of Howard Hughes' colossal flying-boat *Spruce Goose*. Unfortunately the machine was too heavy to fly. It barely made it into the air on its one and only flight and covered a distance less than ten times its own wingspan.

When Alcock and Brown flew across the Atlantic in 1919, their travelling companions were two stuffed cats.

Charles Lindbergh took only four sandwiches with him on his famous transatlantic flight.

Nearly 100 different airlines operate at Heathrow.

The regular scheduled flight between the Orkney Islands of Westray and Papa Westray takes less than two minutes. The check-in time is 20 minutes.

American Airlines saved an estimated $40,000 in 1987 by removing one olive from each salad served in first-class.

Pilot Douglas Corrigan took off in dense fog from New York in 1938 with the intention of flying west to California. However he mistakenly flew east for 28 hours and ended up in Ireland!

Every day, three million passports are checked at airports and border crossings throughout the world. If all these passports were piled up on top of each other, they would form a column higher than Mount Everest.

At 91 square miles, Saudi Arabia's King Khalid International Airport is twice the size of Paris.

Concorde can fly between London and Singapore in the time it took an 18th-century stagecoach to travel from London to Colchester.

All At Sea

Built in England in 1863, the SS *Connector* was constructed in three sections, loosely hinged together. The idea was that the ship's undulating motion would allow it to tackle heavy seas. It was arguably the weirdest vessel ever made.

When the *Royal Adelaide* was driven ashore on Dorset's Chesil Beach in 1875, her cargo of spirits was washed on to the beach. Six people drowned in the wreck, but another 20 died from drinking too much of the washed-up cargo.

In the early 19th century, insanity in the Royal Navy was seven times the national average. This was thought to be due to drunken sailors banging their heads in the confined space between decks.

The famous liner the *Queen Mary* should have been called the *Queen Victoria*. Prior to the launch in 1934, Sir Thomas Royden, a director of shipbuilders Cunard, asked King George V for permission to call the new liner the *Queen Victoria*. But Royden made his request in rather flowery language, asking whether the vessel could be named "after the greatest queen this country has ever known". The king misunderstood and answered: "That is the greatest compliment ever paid to my wife. I shall ask her." The king's wife, Queen Mary, was suitably flattered, leaving Cunard with no choice but to amend its plans.

King James I was a passenger in the first submarine. Designed by Dutchman Cornelius van Drebbel, it had a wooden frame covered with greased leather to make it watertight, and was fitted with oars. Van Drebbel managed to row 15 ft below the surface of the River Thames.

During the Second World War, a German U-boat was sunk by a truck. After attacking a convoy of ships in the Atlantic, the U-boat rose to the surface to see the result of its actions. But the merchant ship it sank had a fleet of trucks on deck, one of which was hurled into the air by the explosion and came crashing down on the surfacing U-boat, breaking the submarine's back.

All gondolas in Venice must be painted black unless they belong to a high-ranking official.

A message in a bottle thrown from the SS *Arawatta* off Queensland, Australia, in 1910 was found washed ashore on nearby Moreton Island 73 years later.

Before sailing from Southampton, the *Titanic* took delivery of 75,000 lb of fresh meat, 25,000 lb of poultry and game, 11,000 lb of fresh fish, 7500 lb of bacon ham, 2500 lb of sausages and 40,000 fresh eggs.

A ship called the *Resolute* once made a 1000-mile journey without any crew. Part of an 1852 expedition which left England in search of the North-West Passage, the *Resolute* was abandoned when it became stuck in ice off the north coast of Canada. The ship was next seen 474 days later by the commander of an American whaler, 1000 miles to the east. Apart from shipping a little water, the *Resolute* was in excellent condition.

The anchor of the *Titanic* weighed 15½ tons and it needed a team of 20 horses to deliver it.

To mark its progress in the 1974 Round the World Yacht Race, the *Adventurer* was given a nine-gun salute by HMS *Endurance* as it rounded Cape Horn. Unfortunately the sixth shot hit the *Adventurer*, severely denting its chances of adding to its victory in the previous leg.

Captain Joshua Slocum, who, in 1898, became the first person to sail solo around the world, was a non-swimmer.

Road Runners

The driver of the first horseless carriage – the steam-driven Fardier – had to stop every 15 minutes to top the boiler up with water.

An act passed in 1865 stated that any self-propelled carriage on an English highway had to have a crew of three, one of whom had to walk in front of the carriage with a red flag to warn horse-drawn vehicles of its approach.

When steam trams first appeared in San Francisco, they terrified horses, causing horse-drawn vehicles to career off in all directions. In a bid to overcome this, an inventor named Matthewson came up with the bright idea of building a steam tram in the shape of a horse.

Early cars didn't have windscreen wipers. Instead drivers rubbed a potato over the glass to help the rainwater run off.

One in 300 of all road accidents in Canada involves a moose.

There's nothing new about attempting to reduce traffic congestion. Julius Caesar tried it 2000 years ago by banning chariots from the centre of Rome.

Hong Kong has the most Rolls-Royces per head of population of any city in the world.

Licensed London taxi cabs are still required by law to carry a bale of hay at all times. The law dates from the days of horse-drawn cabs, but it has never been repealed.

The Maharajah of Nabha once owned a Rolls-Royce customized in the shape of a swan.

Derbyshire farmer George Shields has created a garden shed capable of speeds of up to 55 mph. By fitting wheels, a quad bike engine, an exhaust and five attractive hanging baskets, he has come up with a hut rod which has raced at Donington Park in competition with other unusual vehicles, such as a motorized bed and an F1 armchair.

There are 60,000 taxi drivers in Mexico City.

When Ford wanted to introduce their Pinto car to Brazil, they had to change the name because "pinto" is slang there for "small male genitals".

The Chevrolet Nova wasn't a big seller in Spain where "no va" means "doesn't go."

The people of Luxembourg own more cars per head than any other country.

During the Second World War, the military production of the Ford Motor Company exceeded that of the whole of Italy.

As a result of the capital's heavy traffic, London taxi drivers average no more than 9 mph.

A Californian woman started driving at the age of 91 after her husband had died. Her licence was renewed in 1976, by which time she was 104.

When a woman from Lancashire passed her driving test in 1988, she was 90 years old.

A Middlesex woman took 330 driving lessons and 48 tests before finally passing in 1987.

In 1966, a 75-year-old Texas man received ten traffic tickets, drove on the wrong side of the road four times, committed four hit-and-run offences, and caused six accidents — all in the space of 20 minutes.

Lawrence of Arabia used a fleet of Rolls-Royces to transport his men when he led the British into battle with the Turks in Syria.

If all the roads in the US were joined together, they would encircle the globe 150 times.

The US interstate highway system requires that one mile in every five must be straight so that these sections can be used as airstrips in times of war or other emergency.

Private cars were banned in Bermuda until 1948.

In Ethiopia, there is only one car for every 1468 people.

The 1500-mile long Alaska Highway was built in just six months. Afraid that Japan might attack via the Aleutian Islands, the Americans enlisted 10,000 engineers from the US Army and 4000 civilians to begin work on the road in the spring of 1942. By building seven and a half miles of road a day through forests and marshes, they finished in November of that year.

There are around 150 million cars in the United States – one for every 140 ft of road.

Cars are forbidden on the Channel Island of Sark.

In 1916, a total of 55 per cent of all the cars in the world were Model T Fords, a record which has never been beaten.

Hitler's Mercedes-Benz cars were so heavily armoured that they could do only three miles to the gallon.

Car airbags explode at 200 mph.

During the 1930s farmers in Canada hitched horses to their cars because they couldn't afford to buy petrol.

The world's widest road is the 12-lane Monumental Axis in Brasilia, capital of Brazil.

A pair of Finns hired a taxi to take them to Spain and back in 1991. The fare came to £9000.

Former traffic policeman William Alexander set out to drive the 15 miles from Hereford to Ross-on-Wye in 1996. Thirty-six hours later, after a 1000-mile drive, he and his wife were found very confused and very lost going the wrong way down the M1 near Barnsley.

It costs more to buy a new car today than it cost Christopher Columbus to equip and undertake three voyages of discovery to the New World.

A traffic jam stretched 109 miles northwards from Lyon in France in 1980.

In 1914 French General Gallieni used a fleet of taxis, the drivers still wearing their caps, to ferry his troops from Paris to the Battle of the Marne.

It used to be against the law to slam a car door in Switzerland.

Elgin Street in Bacup, Lancashire, is just 17 ft long.

A mix-up between the accelerator and the clutch caused Mrs. Beatrice Park to drive into the River Wey at Guildford during her 1969 driving test. She and the examiner were rescued after climbing on to the car roof. The examiner was sent home in a state of shock. When Mrs Park asked officials whether she had passed, she was told: "We cannot say until we have seen the examiner's report."

Helen Ireland of Auburn, California, failed her driving test in the first few seconds when she drove straight into the wall of the test centre.

A Frenchman named Huret came up with a 19th-century tricycle that was powered by three dogs. Treadmills were fitted inside the two huge rear wheels and these were driven by the revolving dogs. The contraption was scrapped following protests from animal-lovers.

Under a law of 1888, every cyclist in Britain had to ring the bell on his bicycle non-stop while the machine was in motion. The law was not abolished until 1930.

The first traffic light system in London was installed in Parliament Square in 1868. Revolving red and green lanterns, illuminated by gas, were manually operated by a police officer. But the set of lights was removed four years later when the gas apparatus exploded, seriously injuring the officer on duty.

Until 1979, the driving test in Egypt simply consisted of driving 20 ft forward and the same distance in reverse.

When parking meters were first introduced in the United States, irate drivers used to behead them with axes.

Almost a quarter of the land area of Los Angeles is taken up by cars. In fact there are at least half a million more cars in Los Angeles than there are people.

Traffic congestion is so bad in Bangkok that drivers are advised to carry food, water and even portable toilets when travelling to work in the city.

Just about the first recorded example of road rage took place in 1876 when a British coachman was fined for whipping a cyclist who had overtaken him.